GLOBAL CMO

GLOBAL
CMO

BEST PRACTICE
IN MARKETING
EFFECTIVENESS
& EFFICIENCY
AROUND THE
WORLD

US $24.95   CAN $26.95

GREG PAULL   SHUFEN GOH

www.mascotbooks.com

Global CMO: Best Practice in Marketing Effectiveness &
Efficiency Around the World

For more information, please contact:
Mascot Books
620 Herndon Parkway #320
Herndon, VA 20170
info@mascotbooks.com

Library of Congress Control Number: 2018901576

CPSIA Code: PBANG0218A
ISBN-13: 978-1-68401-848-2

Printed in the United States

CONTENTS

PREFACE

"It's like this; I can tell my sixteen-year-old daughter, 'Don't drink. Don't smoke.' But in the end, I don't know if she will do what I tell her."

And just like that, the challenges of global marketing are laid bare. This quote from one of the global Chief Marketing Officers (CMOs) in this book relates to the challenges of aligning talent and ideas on a global basis under a single worldview. As parents and as consultants, we can relate. The future of global marketing is no longer about a top-down dictatorship, nor is it every man and woman for themselves. One of the messages of this book is collaboration: with internal stakeholders, with consumers and customers, with marketing partners, and with "frenemies" Google and Facebook.

Finding the right collaborative path for your own company has never been harder. In this book, we aim to share the journeys of others.

With the rise of digital media, marketing is moving farther and farther away from its traditional silos every year. It's no longer applicable to talk about a country-specific or regional marketing strategy. Digital transformation has led to fully integrated global strategies, and we felt it was important to write a book that analyzed this change from the perspective of those leading the charge—the global Chief Marketing Officer.

R3, a global marketing consultancy focused on return on media, return on agencies, and return on investment, has been working with CMOs across the globe since 2002. Through the years, the role of marketing in driving innovation within an organization and having a positive, traceable influence on business has grown dramatically. The purpose of this book is to lay out the results of our conversations with global CMOs about the challenges that digital transformation is bringing to both the marketing operation and their specific industries, as well as what will be necessary for future success.

In the following chapters, we explore how digital trends such as e-commerce, martech, adtech, big data, and shifting agency models are shaping CMOs' global strategies, as well as how they are dealing with competition, disruption, and building a learning organization for the future. In the telling of these stories, we reference real-world examples and insights from the major global brands that participated in the development of this book. These brands contributed their insights and wisdom through face-to-face interviews that informed our perspective and guided our research when writing this book.

We were very fortunate to sit down with 18 global CMOs, including Andres Kiger, Vice President of Marketing for Global Partner Markets of Converse; Andrew Clarke, Chief Marketing and Customer Officer of Mars; Axel Schwan, former Executive Vice President and Global CMO of Burger King and current Global CMO of Tim Hortons (he switched over during the process of writing this book); David Roman, CMO of Lenovo; David Timm, Chief Brand Officer of Pizza Hut; Francisco Crespo, SVP and Chief Growth Officer of Coca-Cola; Jennifer Breithaupt, Global Consumer CMO of Citi; Juliana Chugg, EVP and Chief Brand Officer of Mattel; Linda Boff, CMO of General Electric (GE); Linda van Schaik, General Manager of Global Customer Marketing and Communications of Shell; Maryam Banikarim, Global CMO of Hyatt Hotels; Meredith Verdone, CMO of Bank of America; Mukul Deoras, Global CMO of Colgate-Palmolive; Peter Nowlan, EVP and Chief Marketing Officer of Four Seasons Hotels and Resorts; Raja Rajamannar, Chief Marketing and Communications Officer of Mastercard; Syl Saller, Chief Marketing and Innovation Officer of Diageo; Theresa Agnew, CMO for North America of GSK Consumer Healthcare; and Younghee (YH) Lee, CMO of Samsung Electronics.

We would like to express our gratitude for everyone who engaged with us in the making of this book, including Monica Liau, Erin Singleton, Estrella Castellanos, and our extended research teams in R3 Beijing and Shanghai. In the following pages, we will address the biggest challenges facing today's CMOs as they embark on their own digital transformation journeys in an increasingly complex marketing landscape. We hope the insights we've gathered here will accurately explain the current state of digital transformation, as well as shed light on the next step in the journey.

Greg Paull
Shufen Goh

MEET THE
CMOs

ANDRES KIGER

VICE PRESIDENT OF MARKETING FOR GLOBAL
PARTNER MARKETS, CONVERSE

Andres Kiger is the Vice President of Marketing for Global Partner Markets at Converse. In this role, he is responsible for setting strategy, creating programs, aligning partners, designing winning retail and digital platforms, and stewarding the brand across 40 critical emerging markets—including India, Russia, Brazil, Mexico, South Africa, and Indonesia.

Kiger joined the company in January 2015 as Vice President of North America. In this role, he led both the marketing strategy and brand management functions, including advertising, brand design, digital, communications, and retail marketing for the region.

Before joining Converse, Kiger was most recently the head of integrated marketing for Coca-Cola Brazil, responsible for the overall marketing operations and a wide array of specialized functions, including creative development, media, digital, promotions, sports and entertainment properties, and events. Andres set direction and oversaw execution in Brazil for the FIFA World Cup 2014 campaign and set the initial strategy for the 2016 Rio de Janeiro Olympics campaign. Prior to his assignment in Brazil, as Senior Director of Integrated Marketing in Coca-Cola China, Andres led the marketing team in developing and executing their campaign for the Beijing Olympics in 2008. He started his marketing career with the beverage giant in the early 2000s in Hong Kong, and has held several positions, including the Director of Global Merchandise for e-vendors, Licensing Director, and Senior Director of Integrated Marketing for Coca-Cola China.

Kiger is the recipient of numerous international marketing awards, including a 2014 Gold Effie for his work with Coca-Cola Brazil. He received an MBA from Georgetown University and a Bachelor's degree from Emory University. Andres is currently very involved in providing leadership to upcoming business students and participates extensively with several universities, including Georgetown, Boston University, and Georgia Tech.

ANDREW CLARKE

CHIEF MARKETING & CUSTOMER OFFICER, MARS

Andrew Clarke is the Chief Marketing and Customer Officer at Mars Incorporated, a $35B family-owned company. Among its portfolio are some of the world's biggest brands, such as Pedigree®, Royal Canin®, Whiskas®, M&M's®, Snickers®, Dove®, Doublemint®, Extra®, Orbit®, Uncle Ben's, and Dolmio®, to name but a few. At this year's Cannes Lions, Mars was the most awarded advertiser reflecting a philosophy of creativity, strong agency partnerships, and an evidence-based approach to marketing.

As a member of the Mars Leadership Team, Clarke has been the driving force behind reshaping Mars' approach to marketing and sales—developing an integrated strategy that leverages the company's powerful brands while building strong relationships with customers across the world.

Embracing digital commerce to reach consumers in new and different ways is one of Clarke's passions, and together with his team, he has been transforming Mars' capabilities to lead the way in an ever-changing, increasingly challenging consumer and retail landscape.

Through this and his previous roles in Mars, Clarke has focused on driving ambitious change that delivers results. Building, engaging, and inspiring diverse teams at all levels has always been at the heart of his approach.

Since joining Mars in 2000 as Category Leadership Director for Chocolate in the UK, Clarke has accumulated leadership experience and increasing P&L responsibility through a wide range of general management roles spanning the company's chocolate, pet care, and food segments. He has also led geographic operations at the country level in the UK and Ireland and was Regional President for pet care in Latin America, based in Sao Paulo Brazil, from 2011 to 2014. In the Latin America role he built a management team that grew market share, exceeded financial goals, and improved the talent pool across the whole region.

Prior to joining Mars, Clarke was at Marks & Spencer PLC where he rapidly progressed through store management to become a Regional Manager.

Living with his family in the UK, Clarke has a keen interest in all sports, particularly cricket as a playing member of Marylebone Cricket Club, and is a life-long supporter of Liverpool FC.

AXEL SCHWAN

FORMER EVP & GLOBAL CHIEF MARKETING OFFICER, BURGER KING (CURRENT GLOBAL CMO, TIM HORTONS)

Having grown up in a family of restaurateurs, Axel Schwan has always been dedicated to delivering a great guest experience. Schwan's journey in the quick service restaurant industry began when he joined the Burger King team in 2011 as the Marketing Director of Germany, Austria, and Switzerland. Quickly advancing in the business, he took on the role of Vice President of Marketing and Communications EMEA in 2012, and then advanced to the role of Global CMO in January 2014.

Prior to joining Burger King, Schwan held several marketing roles at Danone Waters, and he began his marketing career at Unilever. Among many other accomplishments, his focus on mouthwatering marketing led him, and his team, to accept the 2017 Cannes Marketer of the Year.

With a knack for crafting one-of-a-kind creative that keeps guests craving more, Schwan joined the Tim Hortons team as Global CMO in November 2017. Today he is focused on supporting and strengthening the iconic Canadian brand as it expands around the world.

DAVID ROMAN

CHIEF MARKETING OFFICER, LENOVO

David Roman is the Chief Marketing Officer at Lenovo, responsible for driving all marketing activities for the global PC and technology corporation. During his time with the company, Lenovo made Interbrand's 100 Best Global Brands list for the first time ever in 2015, and earned the honor again in 2016 and 2017—a culmination of the company's brand, PR, and social efforts led by Roman.

Prior to joining Lenovo, Roman was Vice President of Worldwide Marketing Communications for HP's Personal Systems Group, responsible for HP's award winning "The Computer is Personal Again" campaign.

Before HP, Roman was VP Corporate and International Marketing at NVIDIA. He also held different marketing leadership roles at Apple Computer in Europe, Asia-Pacific, and the US. His last Apple role was Vice President of Worldwide Advertising and Brand Marketing.

Roman has been named in the Top 50 Most Influential CMOs (*Forbes*), 100 Most Influential Communicators (The Holmes Report), 50 Most Creative People (Creativity), "Marketing Top 50" (*Ad Age*), and Internationalist 100.

Roman graduated with a degree in architecture and industrial design from the Queensland University of Technology (Australia) after starting his architectural studies at the Polytechnic of Torino (Italy). He also pursued executive MBA studies at INSEAD in Paris.

DAVID TIMM
CHIEF BRAND OFFICER, PIZZA HUT

David Timm is an award-winning international marketing executive whose experience includes market research, trade marketing, brand marketing, advertising, and consulting. He has worked in multicultural environments for and with large multinationals in the US, UK, Africa, Asia, and Eastern/Western Europe.

Timm has held various executive marketing positions with YUM! He has recently moved into the Chief Marketing Capability Officer role for Collider (YUM!'s in-house strategic/brand consultancy) to focus on developing/launching the new *Sales Overnight and Brand Over Time* curriculum to grow marketing capability across all brands. Prior to this role, Timm served as the Chief Brand Officer for Pizza Hut International and was responsible for the full marketing function, asset design, and food/new-product innovation which included digital transformation, sales performance, and brand health in over 100 countries. The company is evolving from a traditional quick-service restaurant (QSR) into an e-commerce business that is both product and service-driven. Prior to that, Timm was CMO for Pizza Hut USA, CMO for KFC in the UK and Ireland, and CMO for KFC in South Africa and Africa.

His advertising experience includes running strategic planning departments and being a member of the management teams for Leo Burnett in Hungary, Seoul, and South Africa. In this time he worked on a diverse number of clients, including Coca-Cola, Mercedes-Benz, McDonald's, Levi's, and Johnnie Walker. In addition to building and leading strategic planning, he was responsible for new business.

Prior to advertising, he was a marketing manager responsible for a beverage portfolio at Bromor Foods (a Cadbury subsidiary) and a brand manager for Hansa Pilsener at South African Breweries, having moved there from AC Nielsen where he began his professional career.

Timm holds an MBA from the Edinburgh Business School and a B Commerce degree from the University of Natal, Republic of South Africa. His professional awards include YUM! Chairman's Award; *Dallas CEO Magazine* CMO Award; and Dallas 500: Most Powerful C-Suite Executives. David was named one of South Africa's top three most influential marketers and has received numerous awards, including Apex Effectiveness, a Cannes Lion, a Clio, the Roger Garlick (Grand Prix), Prism, IPRA, a London International Awards Show, Loeries, and Creative Circle ads of the month.

FRANCISCO CRESPO

SVP & CHIEF GROWTH OFFICER, COCA-COLA

Francisco Crespo is Senior Vice President and Chief Growth Officer of The Coca-Cola Company. A 28-year company veteran, Crespo leads the company's integrated global marketing, corporate strategy, and customer and commercial leadership teams with a clear mandate for driving global growth.

Previously he served as President of The Coca-Cola Company's Mexico business unit based in Mexico City. In this role, Crespo led the company's operations across its second-largest global market, including coordinating a seven-year $8.2 billion system investment plan with local Coca-Cola bottlers. Crespo also has served as President of the South Latin business unit, where he managed company operations in Argentina, Bolivia, Chile, Paraguay, Peru, and Uruguay; as Vice President of Operations for the Brazil business unit, where he led the turnaround of the business, promoting one of the most profitable commercial systems in the region; as General Manager in Chile, where he led the strategy to compete and win against price brands; and as Commercial Director of Coca-Cola FEMSA in Buenos Aires, where he developed several programs that later were exported globally, both on value-based relationships for customers, as well as on segmentation, revenue growth management, and flawless execution. He joined the company in 1989 in Ecuador.

Crespo has served as President of the Coca-Cola Foundation in Chile; Director of AmCham (American Chamber) in Chile; Vice President of AmCham in Argentina; Director of the Lincoln School Association of the Fulbright Foundation; and as a member of the Young Presidents' Organization. Crespo also served as a board member at Embotelladora Andina, a Coca-Cola bottling partner in Chile, Brazil, Argentina, and Paraguay, and J.R. Lindley, the Coca-Cola bottling partner in Lima, Peru. He also has served as a board member at Zurich and Zurich Compañía de Seguros, S.A. (Zurich Insurance's business in Mexico).

An industrial engineer, Crespo graduated from Universidad de Los Andes in Colombia. He has also specialized in areas such as finance, marketing, leadership, and general management, through several programs in prestigious universities and institutions across the world, including the Harvard Business School General Management Program.

JENNIFER BREITHAUPT

GLOBAL CONSUMER CHIEF MARKETING OFFICER, CITI

Jennifer Breithaupt is Global Consumer Chief Marketing Officer at Citi, where she oversees a team focused on crafting distinctive, impactful campaigns that differentiate Citi's industry leading card products and driving long-term brand loyalty with Citi card members across the globe.

As part of her role, Breithaupt leads Citi's entertainment access program, Private Pass, which brings card members closer to their favorite artists through curated offerings and VIP experiences (lounge access, exclusive meet and greets, etc.). Through Private Pass, Citi offered card members access to more than 12,000 events in 2017 alone with the world's biggest artists, including Katy Perry, Lady Gaga, Guns N' Roses, Metallica, Sting, The Chainsmokers, and more.

In recent years, she has spearheaded several successful multi-year partnerships, including the Citi Concert Series on *TODAY* with NBC and Live Nation Entertainment.

Breithaupt is a frequent speaker at industry events and has been widely quoted in media outlets, including *The New York Times, Forbes, Ad Age, Los Angeles Times*, and CMO.com. Recently, Breithaupt was named Billboard's Branding Executive of the Year.

JULIANA CHUGG

EVP & CHIEF BRAND OFFICER, MATTEL

Juliana Chugg serves as EVP and Chief Brand Officer at Mattel, a position she has held since September 2015. With oversight of all aspects of portfolio and strategy, margin management, creative execution, and product development across all of Mattel's global consumer brands, Juliana's portfolio is vast and includes iconic brands, such as Barbie, Hot Wheels, Fisher Price, American Girl, and Thomas the Tank Engine. She works closely with globally licensed partners, such as Disney, Universal, Warner Bros., Nickelodeon, and WWE.

Prior to joining Mattel, Chugg held several senior leadership positions with General Mills, Inc., a multinational manufacturer and marketer of branded consumer foods, where she was a proven leader in operating multi-branded portfolios. Most recently, she served as President of the company's Meals division, which included brands such as Progresso, Old El Paso, and Betty Crocker, where she managed all aspects of the multi-billion dollar business. She also served as President of the company's Pillsbury division. During her time at General Mills, she had a proven track record of driving growth in sales and earnings.

A longtime member of the Board of Directors of the VF Corporation, one of the world's largest and most diverse apparel companies, Chugg holds considerable fashion and apparel industry experience, serving on multiple board committees.

Chugg was born in the UK and her family immigrated to Australia when she was three years old. Chugg attended the University of South Australia in Adelaide, where she earned a Bachelor of Business Administration degree with a concentration in marketing. Chugg relocated to the US in 2004 to join General Mills headquarters.

LINDA BOFF

CHIEF MARKETING OFFICER, GE

Linda Boff is GE's Chief Marketing Officer, leading all global marketing, brand, content, digital, sponsorship, and customer experience for the company. In her role, Boff drives the positioning of GE, one of the world's most powerful brands, as the preeminent digital industrial company, leading industry with software-defined machines and solutions that are connected, responsive, and predictive.

Under Boff's leadership, GE's marketing campaigns and fresh approach to media and content have driven immense results in brand value and recruitment efforts. GE has been recognized as *AdWeek*'s hottest digital marketer and won a coveted Cannes Grand Prix Award in 2016.

Passionate about all things digital and the future of media, Boff is recognized as one of today's most influential CMOs. She is a 2016 Matrix Award winner, CDO Club's 2016 US Chief Digital Officer of the Year, and number five on *Business Insider*'s 50 Most Innovative CMOs list, among other accolades. Boff is also Vice Chair of the Ad Council and a member of Association of National Advertisers executive committees and Marketing 50.

Boff is on the Board of Dunkin' Brands Group, Inc., the parent company of Dunkin' Donuts and Baskin-Robbins, and is Executive Vice President for Partnership with Children, a NYC-based organization which provides social support to hard-to-reach school children.

Previously, Boff was GE's Executive Director of Global Brand Marketing. She also served as CMO of iVillage Properties, part of NBC Universal. Boff joined GE in early 2004 with 18 years of experience in marketing, advertising, and communications, including senior roles at Citigroup, the American Museum of Natural History, and Porter Novelli.

Boff earned a BA in political science and psychology from Union College. She lives in Irvington, New York, with her husband and two children.

LINDA VAN SCHAIK

GENERAL MANAGER, GLOBAL CUSTOMER
MARKETING & COMMUNICATIONS, SHELL

Linda van Schaik started her career at an FMCG company, where she held several sales and marketing roles, the last one being Commercial Manager for the health food business.

After ten years with the FMCG company, she joined Shell Retail in 2008, which is the branch of Shell that runs the petrol service stations. Since joining, she has held various roles in the marketing function with increasing geographical and functional scope. One such position was General Manager for Retail in Benelux and France, where she ran a business with 1,000 outlets that operate 24 hours a day, seven days a week. This role gave Van Schaik some valuable operational experience.

After nearly five years in that role, she moved into her current position of General Manager, Global Customer Marketing and Communications for Shell's Retail and Lubricants Divisions. Van Schaik's team is based in 15 different countries. They are supporting businesses in 70 countries, and she is responsible for setting the strategic direction of her business units.

Van Schaik is the proud mother of two teenage daughters. She is of Dutch nationality and studied marketing in the Netherlands. Above all, she is a passionate retail expert. She loves the dynamics of an environment with high numbers of customers and with various areas for potential growth.

MARYAM BANIKARIM

GLOBAL CHIEF MARKETING OFFICER, HYATT HOTELS

Maryam Banikarim is the Global Chief Marketing Officer at Hyatt Hotels Corporation where she is responsible for helping Hyatt become the most preferred hospitality brand—driving loyalty and community among high-end travelers with a portfolio of 12 global brand experiences. Known for her boundless curiosity, and her ability to build dynamic teams, and forge powerful partnerships, she is a force for change.

Most recently she was the first Chief Marketing Officer at the Gannett Company, responsible for national sales, company-wide marketing, communications, and research. Prior to Gannett, she was Senior Vice President at NBC Universal and Chief Marketing Officer for Univision Communications, Inc. Before that, Banikarim founded a strategy firm, consulting for such clients as Deutsche Bank, Bacardi, and Time-Warner. She also worked at Turner Broadcasting, MacMillan Publishing, and was a lead team member for the launch of Citysearch, an early internet start-up. Banikarim began her career in account management at Young & Rubicam.

Her achievements have been widely recognized: The *New York Post*'s "50 Most Powerful Women in NYC;" *Fast Company*'s "Fast Fifty" list of corporate trailblazers and trendsetters; *Fast Company*'s "Top 10 Disrupters;" *Crain*'s *New York Business* and *Advertising Age*'s "40 under 40;" *Advertising Age*'s "Women to Watch;" *Fast Company*'s "Most Creative People in Business 1000;" and *Adweek*'s "Changing the Game" list of advertising women of New York, as a 2015 Brand Innovator.

Additionally, she is recognized as a Woman of Distinction by the League of Women Voters of the City of New York and was honored by the Girl Scouts Council of Greater New York. She serves on the boards of the Association of National Advertisers, Reporters Without Borders, Columbia University's Alumni Association, and Advertising Week. She is also a member of The Chicago Network.

Banikarim earned both her MBA and Masters of International Affairs from Columbia University and received her undergraduate degree from Barnard College, where she was a Harry S. Truman scholar.

Banikarim resides in Chicago with her husband, two teenage children, and their dog, Charlie.

MEREDITH VERDONE

CHIEF MARKETING OFFICER, BANK OF AMERICA

Meredith Verdone is Chief Marketing Officer at Bank of America and is responsible for all brand strategy and consumer affluent and high net worth marketing across the corporation. Verdone oversees all marketing efforts for the bank's 47 million client relationships, 20,000 retail financial centers and ATM locations, and 14,000 client advisors. She also leads all paid media strategy, creative development, and consumer research and insights.

Verdone started with Bank of America in 1999. During her 18 years of leadership at the company, she has built a team of marketers focused on keeping the brand and the business relevant and competitive. She's led the team in forming new, innovative partnerships, such as Khan Academy on financial education through Better Money Habits. Verdone was also responsible for the 2013 rollout of the global brand platform that unified the company across all divisions domestically and globally with the tagline, "Life's better when we're connected."

Under her leadership, Verdone's team has earned a number of industry accolades, including awards from the Financial Communications Society, the Advertising Research Foundation, and the prestigious Cannes Lions.

Verdone represents the company as its Executive Sponsor for Bank of America's Leadership, Education, Advocacy, and Development (LEAD) for Women Boston Chapter. She has also served as a senior faculty member at the Consumer Bankers Association's Graduate School of Retail Bank Management, and currently serves on the Executive Board for the Ad Council and the Board of Directors for the ANA. She is also a member of a number of industry organizations, including the *Wall Street Journal*'s CMO Network.

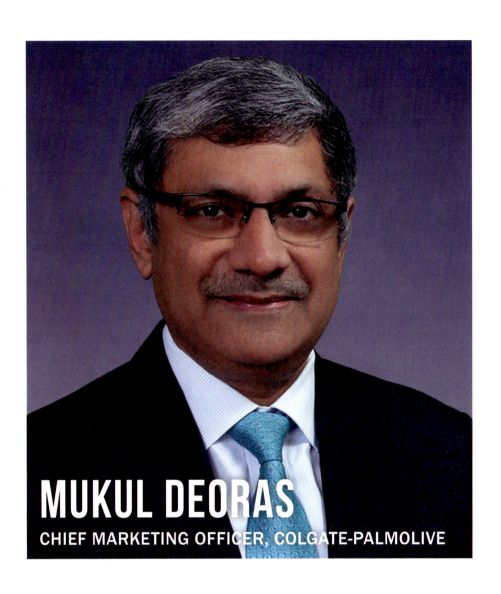

MUKUL DEORAS
CHIEF MARKETING OFFICER, COLGATE-PALMOLIVE

Mukul Deoras is Chief Marketing Officer for the Colgate-Palmolive Company.

Deoras joined Colgate-Palmolive in 2004 as Director, Special Projects for the Asia-Pacific division. Later that year he became Marketing Director Colgate-Palmolive Thailand, and in 2006 he became General Manager.

In 2008, Deoras was promoted to Vice President, Personal Care in Global Marketing, responsible for managing and driving growth for Colgate-Palmolive's personal care worldwide.

In 2010, Deoras became Vice President/General Manager of Colgate-Palmolive India.

In 2012, Deoras became President, Colgate-Palmolive Asia Division where his business insights and focus on building leading brands have contributed significantly to the company's strong volume and sales performance.

In 2015, Deoras was promoted to his current role as Chief Marketing Officer. Deoras is responsible for all the global categories and brands as well as Global Insights, Global Advertising, and Shopper Marketing on a worldwide basis.

Deoras earned his postgraduate degree from the Indian Institute of Management Ahmedabael, India. Prior to Colgate-Palmolive, Deoras worked for Unilever in India.

PETER NOWLAN

EVP & CHIEF MARKETING OFFICER, FOUR SEASONS
HOTELS AND RESORTS

Peter Nowlan is Executive Vice President and Chief Marketing Officer at Four Seasons Hotels and Resorts, setting the global sales and marketing strategies that strengthen Four Seasons' position as the world's leading luxury hospitality company.

Drawing on more than 25 years of marketing experience, including senior leadership roles with globally recognized food, beverage, and restaurant brands, Nowlan is responsible for ensuring a consistent Four Seasons brand experience across all consumer touchpoints. He oversees brand marketing, fourseasons.com, and digital ecosystem, public relations, social media, marketing communications, and advertising, as well as the company's worldwide sales force and central reservations organization.

Prior to joining Four Seasons, Nowlan was Chief Brand and Marketing Officer at Tim Hortons Inc., where he was responsible for all brand, marketing, and research and development (R&D) initiatives.

Previously, Nowlan was Chief Commercial Officer for Molson Coors Canada where he led sales and marketing activity for Molson Coors' world-class portfolio of more than 20 beer brands. This appointment followed four years serving as the organization's Chief Marketing and Strategy Officer, as well as 17 years with Kraft Foods where he held senior leadership roles throughout Canada, the US, and the Asia-Pacific region.

Nowlan holds a Bachelor of Arts in economics and political science from the University of Toronto and an MBA from McMaster University.

RAJA RAJAMANNAR

CHIEF MARKETING & COMMUNICATIONS OFFICER,
MASTERCARD

Raja Rajamannar is Chief Marketing and Communications Officer of Mastercard and President of its healthcare business. He is responsible for building the Mastercard brand, driving business, and advancing sustainable competitive edge for the company.

Rajamannar joined Mastercard in 2013, bringing with him more than 25 years of extensive experience as a global executive managing large P&Ls, as well as business transformation and innovation for companies in multiple industries, including consumer products, financial services, and healthcare.

Prior to Mastercard, Rajamannar served as Chief Transformation Officer of the health insurance firm Anthem (formerly WellPoint). He helped craft the company's new business direction and strategy, managed its $11 billion Medicare Advantage business, and led its $5 billion acquisition of Amerigroup. He had also served as Chief Executive, International, and Chief Innovation and Marketing Officer at Humana.

Earlier, Rajamannar held a number of leadership roles during 15 years with Citigroup, including Global Chief Marketing Officer, Cards and Payments, and Chairman and CEO, Diners Club North America. He has held senior executive leadership positions all over the globe—in North America, Europe, Asia, and MEA. Before that, he spent seven years with Unilever in sales and product management roles. He began his career with Asian Paints in India.

Rajamannar has been globally recognized for the innovative thinking and leadership in business transformation he has brought to executive roles across industries. He has been named one of the "World's Most Influential CMOs" by *Forbes* magazine twice, ranking number nine on the publication's list in 2017.

He is a member of the Board of Directors of PPL Corporation, a Fortune 500 power generation and utilities company, and Cintrifuse, a Cincinnati-based public/private start-up catalyst organization. He serves on the boards of the Ad Council, the Association of National Advertisers, and the New York City Ballet.

Rajamannar received a Master of Business Administration degree from the Indian Institute of Management, in Bangalore, India, and a Bachelor of Technology degree in Chemical Engineering from Osmania University in Hyderabad, India.

SYL SALLER
CHIEF MARKETING & INNOVATION OFFICER, DIAGEO

Syl Saller is the Chief Marketing Officer for Diageo and a member of Diageo's Executive Committee. Diageo is the world's leading premium drinks business operating in 180 countries with over 400 brands, including Johnnie Walker, Smirnoff, Captain Morgan, Tanqueray, and Guinness. Saller oversees all Global Marketing, Design, Innovation, the Futures Group, and Reserve, Diageo's luxury division.

Before she was appointed CMO, she was Global Innovation Director, responsible for Diageo's innovation strategy, including all new product development, launch programs, and R&D. Prior to that, she was Marketing Director for Diageo Great Britain.

Saller joined Diageo in 1999 from Allied Domecq Retail where she was Marketing Development Director on the Executive Board. She started her career in brand management with Gillette, holding both US and global roles, before moving to the Holson Burnes Group, where she was General Manager of the Holson Division.

Saller is President of the Marketing Society, a member of the 30% Club, Marketing Group of Great Britain (MGGB), and Women in Advertising and Communications, London (WACL). She is consistently recognized by external organizations as a leader and expert in her field, recently being recognized as one of *Campaign Magazine*'s five most influential Global CMOs. She was named Marketer of the Year, one of the 500 Most Influential People in Britain, *Forbes* Top 50 CMOs, and *Ad Age*'s Women to Watch. Saller has been a Non-Executive Director of Domino's Pizza Group where she chaired the nominations committee and served on the RemCo.

Saller graduated summa cum laude from the University of New Hampshire and holds an MBA from the Harvard Business School. She is married to her husband, Roger, and has two children, Alexa and Jake.

THERESA AGNEW

**CHIEF MARKETING OFFICER, NORTH AMERICA,
GSK CONSUMER HEALTHCARE**

In her role since 2014, Theresa Agnew oversees the brand and portfolio strategy for GSK Consumer Healthcare in the US, leveraging traditional trade channels as well as new media and technology. She leads the marketing organization as they activate growth plans targeting consumers, customers, and healthcare professionals.

Agnew has been instrumental in leading the digital transformation for GSK's US Marketing division, returning the US smokers health division to growth, launching Flonase as an Rx to OTC switch, continuing the momentum of strong growth in oral care, and leading an increased focus on talent development, capability building, and career progression for GSK's marketing in the US.

Prior to joining GSK, Agnew served as Senior Vice President, US Marketing for Essilor of America, and also spent over 20 years with Johnson & Johnson, where she worked in positions of increasing and varied responsibility in marketing and sales across multiple operating divisions and multiple global geographies.

YOUNGHEE LEE

CHIEF MARKETING OFFICER, SAMSUNG ELECTRONICS

Younghee (YH) Lee joined Samsung Electronics as the Vice President of the Global Marketing Group of Samsung's Mobile Communications business in July 2007. Since then, she has played a pivotal role in making the Samsung Galaxy one of the most beloved smartphone brands in the world. In 2012, she was promoted to Executive Vice President and has continued to strengthen the Samsung Galaxy brand through this position. Appointed Chief Marketing Officer in 2017, she now also leads the Global Marketing Center, overseeing all products and corporate marketing strategies, including mobile devices, home appliances, and TVs.

Lee is a veteran of the consumer industry, having spent over 18 years working for multinational global FMCG companies. Prior to her current position at Samsung, Lee was the Managing Director of two business divisions for L'Oréal Korea, the world's leading cosmetics company that encompasses Lancôme and L'Oréal Paris. During her time at L'Oréal, she held several key positions and contributed to the exponential growth of the company. Before L'Oréal, Lee acted as Marketing Manager for Unilever Korea.

Lee earned a Bachelor of Arts degree with a major in English Literature and a minor in Mass Communication from Yonsei University in 1987. In 1989, Lee graduated with a Master of Science degree in advertising from the Medill School of Journalism at Northwestern University and attended the INSEAD L'Oréal Joint MBA executive course in 2001.

GLOBAL CMO

DIGITAL TRANSFORMATION AND THE CMO

TODAY'S DIGITAL LANDSCAPE

In a world of 3.5 billion internet users, we are no longer facing a digital future. We are in the midst of its renaissance. This has opened the door to a whole new mindset that global CMOs must allow to reshape their teams, their ethos, and their businesses in order to fully and effectively traverse these new global business frontiers.

Over the past five years, the internet has continued to transform the way businesses reach out to consumer markets. Two-thirds of the world's internet users are now based in the developing world,[1] opening access to new target demographics. Additionally, the mobile phone has become a device constantly at the fingertips of these billions of prospective customers and is now the most popular tool used to browse the internet. *"When you look at all the data, the amount of time people are spending with digital media is increasing. We know that everything is mobile now; the amount of mobile adoption is just so significant. When they're in mobile they're on social, so social and mobile are becoming interchangeable terms,"* says Meredith Verdone, Chief Marketing Officer of Bank of America. According to Cisco Systems,[2] mobile data traffic will increase globally sevenfold between 2016 and 2021.

The way we consume information also continues to develop, with video set to account for 82 percent of global internet traffic by 2021. Technology is making the world a smaller place with each passing year. Andres Kiger, Vice President of Marketing for Global Partner Markets at Converse echoes this sentiment.

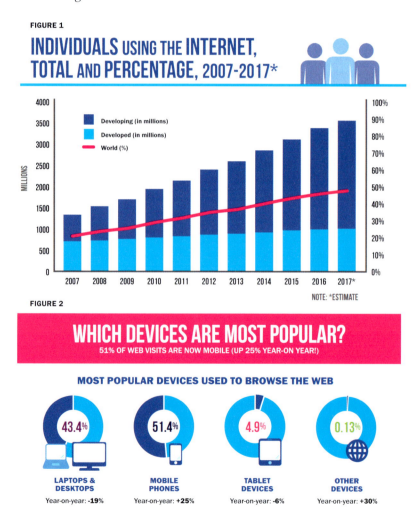

FIGURE 1

INDIVIDUALS USING THE INTERNET, TOTAL AND PERCENTAGE, 2007-2017*

- Developing (in millions)
- Developed (in millions)
- World (%)

MILLIONS

NOTE: *ESTIMATE

FIGURE 2

WHICH DEVICES ARE MOST POPULAR?
51% OF WEB VISITS ARE NOW MOBILE (UP 25% YEAR-ON YEAR!)

MOST POPULAR DEVICES USED TO BROWSE THE WEB

43.4%	51.4%	4.9%	0.13%
LAPTOPS & DESKTOPS	**MOBILE PHONES**	**TABLET DEVICES**	**OTHER DEVICES**
Year-on-year: **-19%**	Year-on-year: **+25%**	Year-on-year: **-6%**	Year-on-year: **+30%**

"One thing that I find interesting is the access to technology that they [the consumers] have across countries, across regions, and even across socio-economic levels." It is not enough for brands to get their name or message in front of audiences. They need to create an interactive, engaging, and memorable experience in order to be heard in a noisy, competitive environment. *"If the '50s and '60s were the golden age of advertising, today is the golden age of creativity: there are more platforms, channels, and formats open to us than ever before,"* says Syl Saller, Chief Marketing and Innovation Officer of Diageo. *"As a marketer, that's tremendously exciting. But among this period of rapid change, what endures and continues to be defining in our industry is the power of film that emotionally connects with people."*

For a global CMO, digital transformation can be a challenge because, in addition to the rapid rate of digital transformation happening in the market, the rate of digital maturity across different markets varies and changes incredibly quickly. *"There's a continuum of transformation underway and it varies by brand and geography,"* says Juliana Chugg, Executive Vice President and Chief Brand Officer of Mattel. *"As we look at our digital quotient in the company, we have markets, such as China, that are the most advanced in terms of a digital-first mindset with digital consumer engagement central to our go-to market strategy."*

THE STATE OF DIGITAL DISRUPTION

All of these developments require a business model that evolves with the times, leveraging the latest technology to address customer needs. Companies like Amazon, Airbnb, Uber, and Google have indelibly changed the playing field and redesigned entire industries. By building their business around customer experience, engagement, and the journey through the digital world, they have effectively altered buyer expectations. Companies are now required to understand the singular and unique wants of their customers and create a tailored experience in response. *"Companies can help their customers become brand advocates by building a brand identity that they can relate to, and also by sharing similar values,"* says YH Lee, Chief Marketing Officer of Samsung. *"Providing an emotional connection is an important part of this process. Despite the differences in digital maturity between markets, human-centered stories and messages are universal, and digital media is the ideal platform to build, share, and amplify this content."*

FIGURE 3

THE FUTURE OF INTERNET USE

It would take an individual more than **5 MILLION YEARS** to watch the amount of video that will cross global IP networks each month in **2021**. Every second, **A MILLION MINUTES** of video content will cross the network by **2021**.

Globally, IP video traffic will be **82%** of all consumer internet traffic by **2021**, up from **73%** in **2016**.

Live internet video will account for **13%** of Internet video traffic by **2021**. Live video will grow **15-FOLD** from **2016** to **2021**.

Globally, mobile data traffic will increase **SEVENFOLD** between **2016 AND 2021**.

In order to compete, companies must welcome the disruption and this new, intimate relationship with their consumer. They must also set a strategy to discover how new tools and expectations fit into their future, as well as recognize that digital transformation is a never-ending journey. *"We have been going through rapid change in the digital space,"* says Theresa Agnew, Chief Marketing Officer for North America of GSK Consumer Healthcare. *"My philosophy is you've never fully transformed in the digital world because everything changes so quickly. We have a solid foundation in terms of how we approach mobile, social, SEO, content, new technology in our US business, but we continuously need to evolve and stay current."*

With the sands of change shifting quickly beneath their feet, any company worth its salt is putting digital transformation and integration goals at the top of the initiatives list. However, merely penciling "digital" into the agenda isn't enough. *"Today, brands fully recognize that digital touchpoints are not an either-or proposition. Digital platforms touch and affect absolutely every single contact point with your consumer. Brands are now fully part of a new digital reality and everything we do is visible: the good and the bad,"* says Andres Kiger of Converse.

Figuring out how to harness the tools that are now available in a way that furthers business goals and enhances brand identity is key. We are swimming in a sea of new information of such vastness and detail that it could hardly be imagined only five years ago. Online access and the ability to track customers from their first brand interaction all the way to the point of conversion gives companies unprecedented access into the consumer mindset. But it's easy to get bogged down in the details. In a report that surveyed 600 respondents,[3] more than half of the organizations have a digital marketing strategy, but only nine percent have had a digital transformation process in place for more than two years, and only half of those companies had completely mapped out the customer journey, meaning many are changing without true customer centricity. *"The challenge for CMOs has always been about engaging consumers. You need a laser focus on understanding your customer and finding new ways to engage and care for them. You have to capitalize on the latest tools and still find ways to connect with consumers emotionally,"* says Maryam Banikarim, Global Chief Marketing Officer of Hyatt Hotels. *"You have to see around corners to identify trends and new opportunities because ultimately, generating growth and profitability comes from listening, adapting, and taking action to meet our customers' needs."*

CASE STUDY

HYATT WORLD OF HYATT

1 **BACKGROUND:** In early 2017, Hyatt Hotels launched the World of Hyatt—Hyatt's new global platform grounded in the simple idea that a little understanding goes a long way. In the face of a hospitality industry completely changed by digital transformation and the disruption caused by non-traditional players, Hyatt's CEO described the World of Hyatt as "a platform powered by our purpose—caring for people so they can be their best—and it inspires how we engage with guests, interact with colleagues and owners, and operate our business. Importantly, it's designed to deepen our relationship with our community beyond traditional hotel stays." The launch was supported by a fully integrated marketing campaign and culminated in the launch of Hyatt's new loyalty program.

2 **PROCESS:** The launch of World of Hyatt was supported by an unprecedented integrated marketing campaign called "For a World of Understanding." The campaign debuted its anthem spot during the 89th Oscars broadcast, and consisted of a series of personal vignettes speaking to the power of understanding. The global campaign was extended across TV, digital, social, out-of-home, in-hotel, print, and events throughout 2017, with a heavy emphasis in the United States, China, and India. The new customer loyalty program launched in March focused on understanding as the guiding principle, and was designed based on listening to consumers' needs and taking action. The new program includes more tiers and more ways to earn status, which allows for more meaningful rewards and benefits for members.

3 **RESULTS:** The launch of World of Hyatt sparked conversations around the power of understanding, brought awareness to cultural barriers, and showed how we can break through them to stand together and unite as one. The Oscars spot was the company's first TV ad since 1985, and at the end of 2017 the spot had nearly 3 million views on YouTube. "For a World of Understanding" saw 929.6mm earned media impressions and 291 earned media placements as well as 60k social mentions and 22.8k engagements.

AGENCY MODELS ARE CHANGING

This drastic change has also led to a shift in the agency model. The way CMOs engage with their agency partners is totally different in the digital age. For many organizations, it's not enough to have a traditional agency roster. Today's marketing teams are bringing in technology vendors, crowdsourcing creative ideas from new platforms, and looking for agencies that didn't exist a decade ago in the e-commerce, digital influencer, and data analytics spaces. As several markets have slowed down in recent years, procurement teams are also playing a larger role in finding and paying agency partners, forcing many agencies to provide more capabilities at a lower cost. This trend, coupled with the emergence of the consulting firms in the marketing mergers and acquisitions (M&A) space, has effectively altered the traditional agency landscape, forcing a change in the way that marketers structure their external relationships in this digital world. Syl Saller of Diageo points out how the shift from traditional to digital media channels has changed the way that CMOs choose agency partners:

In 1997 when Diageo was formed, the industry was still broadly dominated by print media, TV, and direct mail. The internet was still in its infancy, with people going "online" to do little more than send an email. Over the last 20 years we've seen the huge fragmentation of media create opportunities to reach people in more occasions through more channels. The competition for people's attention has never been fiercer, and it's creativity that makes the difference. And I mean all kinds of creativity—in the content, in the way you use media, in the partners you choose.

THE CHALLENGES FACING THE GLOBAL CMO

The age of digital disruption and innovation has put the marketing industry in a state of constant flux. Set firmly in the center of this rapidly changing landscape, CMOs can often struggle to lead their organization on a course of integration and digital transformation. *"I would say digital transformation is probably our single biggest challenge. It's not the transformation that is the challenge but how the new world of performance marketing will integrate with traditional marketing and where it will balance out and settle down. It's probably the single biggest thing that we're dealing with,"* says David Timm, Chief Brand Officer of

Pizza Hut. At the same time, the responsibility for transforming the business and rising to customer expectations lies heavily on the shoulders of these same CMOs and their teams. Based on a recent survey by the Altimeter Group,[4] digital transformation and integration is largely led by the CMO, not the Chief Information Officer (CIO) or Chief Technology Officer (CTO), and it is well known that by 2018, the CMO's technology expenditure will exceed the CIO's.

FIGURE 4

EXECUTIVES CHAMPIONING DIGITAL TRANSFORMATION EFFORTS

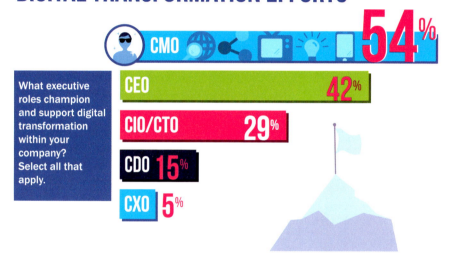

What executive roles champion and support digital transformation within your company? Select all that apply.

- CMO 54%
- CEO 42%
- CIO/CTO 29%
- CDO 15%
- CXO 5%

This is a tricky spot to be in—at the apex of a changing marketing world and in a company that is working to understand how new digital technologies relate to their business. Some organizations become mixed up, failing to define a clear and simple focus. In the eyes of successful global CMOs, it is keeping a spotlight on customer experience and engagement that is key to future achievements. *"Before we think about digital as a brand, and as a business, we always try to get to a place where we understand our guests from every angle…,"* says Axel Schwan, the former Executive Vice President and Global Chief Marketing Officer of Burger King. *"From there we can identify how technology can help to improve the relevance of our brand and make our guests even happier. That might sound simple, but we like to keep things very, very simple—we just want to make our guests happy. Which means, first and foremost, that we cannot forget about delivering on the basics."*

NAVIGATING THE NEW CONSUMER JOURNEY

Today, it is a fact that Chief Executive Officers (CEOs) and CMOs are more likely to be in charge of driving customer experience, putting it at the forefront of their business strategies. *"Now there's a greater emphasis on the entire relationship with the consumer. We are constantly testing, learning, making mistakes, getting back on the horse again, scraping past beliefs, and learning all over again,"* says Andres Kiger of Converse. In a survey of 500 digital transformation strategists and executives, 55 percent cited "evolving customer behaviors and preferences" as the primary catalyst for change.[5] Yet, one of the top challenges facing these executives is understanding the behavior or impact of the new customer. If the digital transformation conversation does not center around understanding customers and their expectations, then it will have little effect on business outcomes.

"Our brand advantage emerges when we serve our consumers better or, simply put, define the job that our brands are doing for our consumers," says Francisco Crespo, Senior Vice President and Chief Growth Officer of Coca-Cola. *"We are evolving the role of digital from simply a better connection node with consumers to enhance the business potential across the value spectrum…market foresights, consumer behavior, e-commerce, manufacturing, sourcing, data-driven analytics, and eventually consumer experience."*

Peter Nowlan, Chief Marketing Officer of Four Seasons Hotels and Resorts, also makes this same point, noting that, particularly in the travel sector, a deep understanding of the consumer will ultimately lead to success. He explains:

I think the travel journey is so holistic that it all links together—from dreaming of a trip to research and decision making, right through to sharing the experience with one's personal network. Four Seasons wants to be there throughout, bringing it all together in a cohesive and satisfying experience for the consumer. The key for us is to deliver a consistent Four Seasons experience, recognizing our guests and their unique preferences and adding value at all points during their travel.

In the midst of this pressure to evolve, the past few years have also seen companies adding new jobs to the traditional C-suite cache, with titles that center around innovation, customer experience, and even growth. This can sometimes edge in on the role of the CMO, causing overlap that can create confusion and perhaps conflict. In order to keep their jobs relevant, the CMO must prove that they are the ones holding the key to the company's digital success, both inside and outside of the marketing function

COMPETITION IN THE C-SUITE

Today's marketing department is about more than simply driving awareness via traditional marketing initiatives. It's about driving a larger organizational shift, as well as fulfilling the customer's purpose. The challenge is moving beyond the antiquated notion of attaining customers to do whatever fulfills the company's purpose. Instead, it is about motivating the company to listen to and fulfill the customer's purpose. In order to achieve this, CMOs need to form a partnership with CEOs to better understand the structure and drive of the business. Twenty years ago, marketing and advertising were focused on product awareness and brand affinity. But now that new technology allows companies to track a consumer across all touchpoints, marketing is as much about driving sales as it is about driving awareness. The expectations for actual, tangible business results are growing, and in order to implement a strategy, one needs to understand how the business works. As the CEO is responsible for driving organizational shifts, the CMO needs to get in and leverage all the information in order to align correctly and shift the entire organization.

It is also key that business models are based on business strategy, competitive advantage, and brand goals. Technology and digital strategies are tools to achieve these things, but they alone do not help connect to consumers, nor do they achieve growth and business goals. Businesses that recognize where the market is heading, understand the opportunities that it presents, and move quickly with sound strategic thinking stand to profit most from digital transformation.

FINDING THE RIGHT TALENT

Digital transformation also requires multidisciplinary involvement, which means having the foresight to effectively restructure teams and hire the right people to fill in the gaps. Linda Boff, Chief Marketing Officer of General Electric, reveals that GE's digital transformation journey began by bringing in new types of talent:

> "The biggest challenge is understanding all of the different components that are the infrastructure of your marketing mix. What do you need to do to be able to use all of them? How do you leverage the data, customer experience, and customer journeys when you have an existing infrastructure in place?"

LINDA VAN SCHAIK
Shell

I would say for us it starts with the business strategy which is to transform GE, the industrial company, into a digital industrial company. With the intent being that the worlds that we live in, the worlds that our customers live in can operate more efficiently, more effectively, and more cost-effectively. Maybe five, six years ago as a strategy, the company decided to make a big play in digital; we opened a software center, we brought on data and all kinds of data entrepreneurs, computer scientists, et cetera.

Today's marketing and advertising ecosystem is so fragmented that no one can be an expert on everything. That being said, at a CMO roundtable focused on exploring digital transformation hosted by R3 in New York City in early 2017, CMOs agreed it is crucial to educate yourself enough to be able to ask the right questions and identify the right talent that can help an organization move toward the future. CMOs today are never going to be as tech-savvy as the digital natives currently entering the job market, but they need to be able to identify the right talent and keep the pace of digital transformation within the organization fast enough to keep the talent engaged and invested in the business.

BATTLING THE LEGACY DISEASE

It is also the role of the CMOs of established brands to drive their company to shake off the "legacy disease" in order to keep up and flourish in this age of digital disruption. For example, the financial sector alone has had to face the rise of mobile payments, blockchain, and other disruptors in recent years. However, most financial institutions' internal information technology (IT) innovations take years to implement, moving much slower than smaller, agile companies. Linda van Schaik, General Manager of Global Customer Marketing and Communications at Shell, points out, *"The biggest challenge is understanding all of the different components that are the infrastructure of your marketing mix. What do you need to do to be able to use all of them? How do you leverage the data, customer experience, and customer journeys when you have an existing infrastructure in place?"*

Going forward, these legacy companies will have to learn from best practice in the industry, like the transformation of GE, and become a champion to disrupt their own processes internally or face becoming obsolete. In order to be an effective CMO and drive growth for the company in today's digital age, it's important to be an agent of change while still keeping business strategy clearly in the mind's eye. *"We have embraced the digital challenge right from the top; from the owners through to the board all the way throughout the business, our digital transformation initiative is hardwired. It's front and center for everyone,"* says Andrew Clarke, Chief Marketing and Customer Officer of Mars. *"How do we reach consumers in new and different ways? How do we convert transactions in new and different ways? How do we add more value in new and different ways, including new business models as well as our existing brands and channels?"*

One key aspect of driving this change is leveraging the new tools afforded to marketing teams by digital transformation. The rise of big data and the incredibly vast ecosystem of technology solutions that are out there have become indispensable to CMOs. The challenge lies in figuring out the most effective way to add these into the marketing mix. Is it better to invest in data analytics or new technologies internally, or engage external partners? These are the questions CMOs must ask themselves to become "Future Fit." David Timm of Pizza Hut shares some challenges his team faced when starting out on their digital journey:

We've probably failed more than we've succeeded. I think the reason we failed is not because it's the wrong thing to do but because we didn't know how to execute well in the new, digital world. While we were shifting to digital channels, we were doing it in a very traditional way. Frankly, because we didn't have the capability or the knowledge to really understand how to optimize the new world of marketing.

For a CMO in this new world, failure isn't necessarily a negative thing. It indicates a willingness to test the digital waters and learn what works and what doesn't. There is no one-size-fits-all strategy when it comes to digital transformation.

FIGURE 5

THE MOST IMPORTANT DIGITAL TRANSFORMATION INITIATIVES RANKED

		VERY IMPORTANT	SOMEWHAT IMPORTANT
	Improving processes that expedite changes to digital properties, ie. website updates, new mobile or social platforms, etc.	80%	19%
	Updating our website and e-commerce programs for a mobile world	71%	25%
	Integrating all social, mobile, web, e-commerce, service efforts, and investments to deliver an integrated and frictionless customer experience	70%	36%
	Updating customer-facing technology systems	66%	29%
	Further research into our customers' digital touch points, as there's more to learn	63%	36%
	Building a social media program that is more competitive against our peers	58%	36%
	Creating a sense of urgency to show executives that our digital transformation effort does not align with current plans	54%	27%
	Overhauling customer service to meet expectations of connected customers	46%	49%

THE FUTURE FIT CMO

The future of digital transformation in marketing will be largely decided by CMOs themselves. There is no roadmap to outline what each organization should do. It's up to every company to figure out how to move forward. *"We're on the journey, we're making tremendous progress, but of course it's challenging. There's no obvious playbook to follow here,"* says Andrew Clarke of Mars. *"There are lots of ideas and thoughts and opinions in the marketplace, and therefore navigating and executing our digital strategy as a large business, with real legacy assets and big brands geographically dispersed, is a massive change management challenge as well."*

Discussing these challenges with the 18 CMOs interviewed for this book led us to develop the Eight Actions of a Future Fit CMO. What do CMOs need to do to ensure that their jobs and influence within their organization remain intact? These eight key ingredients, many coming directly from the CMOs themselves, shed light on how marketing leaders can become future proof, ensuring they will continue to have a prominent seat at the C-suite table. Throughout the process of writing this book, we learned that despite each industry's individual challenges, there are common threads that connect CMOs around the world. Certain truths about being a global marketer in today's landscape ring true across the board, and there are lessons to be learned from each of these CMOs' stories that can be applied to nearly every marketing leader's strategy.

We hope you enjoy the insights gleaned from these conversations, and learn something about building a modern marketing playbook along the way.

TAKING ON THE COMPETITION

Chief Marketing Officers are facing two types of competition in today's landscape. The first is external competition, or the competition facing the organization in terms of market share and business results. In this wave of digital disruption, most organizations are facing competitors that they didn't have ten years ago—Airbnb challenging traditional hotels, Venmo and Apple Pay challenging big banks, and online streaming services challenging traditional cable companies. The second form of competition is internal, or the challenges posed to CMOs by the rise of new C-suite executives as organizations struggle to build digital capabilities and own their consumer journey.

THE EVOLUTION OF THE COMPETITIVE LANDSCAPE

While this advent of digital disruption may seem sudden, the movement can be traced back to 1995, when the term first popped up in the *Harvard Business Review*[1] as "a process whereby a smaller company with fewer resources is able to successfully challenge established incumbent businesses." Back then, it was the music, photography, and video rental sectors that were feeling the burn from digital start-ups like MySpace, Apple, and Google. Fifteen years later, digital innovation advanced in another wave, and the print media, television, and travel industries were shaken up by Airbnb, streaming videos, and travel websites. *"Media was one of the first industries to be disrupted largely because, at the time, media companies gave away their content for free on the internet without recognizing the value they were giving away. Once that genie was out of the bottle, there was no going back,"* says Maryam Banikarim of Hyatt Hotels. *"Disruption comes fast and furious. And it comes when you don't expect it. Just look at what's happening in retail today. So we are on the lookout, as much as we can be, for disruption to come our way too."*

FIGURE 6

WAVES OF DIGITAL DISRUPTION

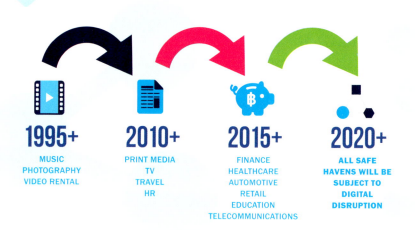

1995+
MUSIC
PHOTOGRAPHY
VIDEO RENTAL

2010+
PRINT MEDIA
TV
TRAVEL
HR

2015+
FINANCE
HEALTHCARE
AUTOMOTIVE
RETAIL
EDUCATION
TELECOMMUNICATIONS

2020+
ALL SAFE
HAVENS WILL BE
SUBJECT TO
DIGITAL
DISRUPTION

Starting in 2015, finance, healthcare, automotive, retail, education, and telecommunications industries found themselves playing catch-up in the face of online banking, Venmo, and even WeChat. *"Digital disruption has certainly been more present,"* says Jennifer Breithaupt, Global Consumer Chief Marketing Officer of Citi. *"Really, for us, mobile banking and the future deployment of omni-channel banking is critical. When you think about using tools like mobile, as well as digital payment tools, social media, video tellers, really all of those things that have more of a self-service model, that's where the disruption has come into place. We've had to really fast-track how people interact with us, how they bank with us, and how we become the bank of the future."*

Even industries that many would assume haven't been affected by digital disruption are feeling the pressure and starting to prepare for the future. *"Disruption is something that we have talked about on many occasions,"* says Linda van Schaik of Shell. *"At the moment, we are seeing certain trends that have caused us to start thinking and testing. Things like car sharing and autonomous driving. These will probably lead to a shift from a B2C [business-to-customer] to B2B [business-to-business] type of customer relationship. It's definitely disruption based on digitalization."*

By 2020, there will be no industry—however stolid, set, or ingrained—that will remain a safe haven from digital disruption. In a survey by Dell of 4,000 business leaders, 78 percent believe digital start-ups pose a threat to their organization now or in the near future, and 62 percent have seen new competitors enter the market as a result of the emergence of digital technology.[2]

"We are actively seeing disruption happening across our entire supply chain, from branding to manufacturing to distribution," says Francisco Crespo of Coca-Cola. *"We are seeing a proliferation of new entrants in the North American Ready to Drink [NARTD] space able to launch and scale at an increasingly fast pace. Traditional barriers to entry are no longer the issue given advancements in data and technology."*

FIGURE 7

DIGITAL COMPETITION AND THE CMO

48% of global businesses don't know what their industry will look like in 3 years

78% of businesses consider digital start-ups a threat, either now or in the future

6/10 Around 6 in 10 businesses are unable to meet customers' top demands

5% Just 5% of businesses can be classed as 'Digital Leaders'

73% confess digital transformation could be more widespread

Peter Nowlan of Four Seasons Hotels and Resorts explains how they have been able to stay ahead of disruption:

Whether we talk about industry consolidation, emerging technologies, or new players in the market, the bottom line is most of these disruptors are grounded in evolving consumer behavior. Our brand belief has always been based on service, the people who deliver that service, and the relationships we have with our guests. Therefore, we've been able to stay ahead of change by sticking to what we know best and using the impact of disruptors to our advantage.

This restructuring of the world business order has been on the horizon for more than two decades and, in order change with the times, brands need to work overtime to cure the "legacy disease" that still seems to affect many companies—especially in established markets like the United States. Many continue to drag their feet, moving slowly (or not at all) to transform internal systems and external practices. These organizations need to adopt the strategy of "learn, unlearn, and relearn," which is crucial for both promoting digital transformation and building sustainable integration. *"The challenge is not the learning curve. The challenge is the 'unlearning' curve,"* says Mukul Deoras, Global Chief Marketing Officer of Colgate-Palmolive. *"To me, that is the biggest hurdle. How do you get off the horse you're riding so that you can get onto another one?"* Many marketers have already taken drastic steps to change internal legacy processes and systems. One of those steps is breaking down internal silos to make sure there is a heightened level of cross-team functionality. *"The old days of 'IT is over here' and 'marketing is over there' and you're fighting and saying, 'Why didn't you bring me in soon enough?' It literally feels like another lifetime to me,"* says Linda Boff of GE.

CHANGING MINDSETS IS KEY

The first step in the transformation is moving away from the mindset that there is a difference between digital and traditional businesses. Eighty percent of the 700 CMOs interviewed in a C-suite study by IBM[3] believe the business landscape will change "to include more digital, virtual interaction in three to five years." Mukul Deoras of Colgate-Palmolive explains, *"My biggest challenge is breaking out of the comfort zone of the old way of doing things—whether they're right or wrong. That comfort came with the knowledge of certain measurements. Those measurements were a crutch on which we based much of our consumer engagement strategy. Very simplistically put, whether a [gross rating point] GRP thrown into the market made a difference wasn't very clear. As they say, half of it worked—we didn't know which half, but we certainly knew that half of it worked—and we just lived with that, as long as we measured enough."*

This is no longer enough. The new reality is that disruptive digital models are popping up across industries. It's not just about competition from digitally native start-ups. Existing suppliers, former partners, and current competitors who are able to use new technologies to augment and fragment the traditional value chain are creating fresh competition from every side, meaning everyone has to innovate in order to even the playing field.

GLOBAL CMOS, DISRUPTED

As industries work to restructure the way their company is arranged and how to define the business, CMOs must also consider how they will evolve their own role within the company to ensure continued relevance within the organizational structure.

In the eyes of Raja Rajamannar, Chief Marketing Officer of Mastercard, the role of today's marketer should be viewed much more within the realm of general manager than the marketers of yesteryear. He explains:

Companies have three big lines of spending: technology, people, and marketing. When CEOs are running short on revenue, they are more likely to pull money from the marketing department because the immediate impact of marketing is not always seen or appreciated by many CEOs. When asked a tough question, because marketing people have come from the creative route, they struggle with numbers. And in that kind of scenario, they lose their credibility. They lose their budgets.

CMOs are also facing new challenges in the C-suite, as new titles crop up in the wake of digital transformation. Some view these new executives as a threat to CMOs because they are encroaching on and overlapping with their established territory. Ten years ago, there were no Chief Digital Officers, Chief Growth Officers, or Chief Experience Officers. However, the rise of the new C-suite executives isn't necessarily a negative for CMOs. For example, at Citi, the Chief Customer and Digital Experience Officer and the CMO's teams work hand in hand. *"It's really important that we stay connected,"* says Jennifer Breithaupt of Citi. *"The good news is we, and our teams, sit very close together, and we are all aligned around the same goals and priorities. It's been a truly amazing, collaborative partnership and one that is critically important as it relates to the end-to-end customer experience."* Others see the rise of these new C-suite executives as a direct conflict with the existing role of the CMO. *"When you have a Chief Digital Officer, Chief Customer Experience Officer, and Chief Revenue Officer, what is marketing supposed to do if they no longer handle any of those components?"* says Raja Rajamannar of Mastercard. *"That is an existential threat to the CMO at one level."* To some extent, it makes sense for CMOs to be a little wary of this new competition, as there are several possible trajectories for the CMO going forward, and not all of them are positive.

UP OR OVER; DOWN AND OUT

As organizations focus on driving growth, *Harvard Business Review* published an article that outlined four possible futures for CMOs: up, over, down, or out.[4] Each of these possible futures has different implications for marketing teams and organizations as a whole. In an upward trajectory situation, CMOs are promoted into new and bigger roles that feature a larger focus on end-to-end consumer experience. For example, KFC's former US CMO was recently promoted to the role of President and Chief Concept Officer, responsible for driving overall strategy and business performance, and reflecting the importance placed on marketing being able to move the business needle.

FIGURE 8

UP: CMOs are promoted into new roles

OVER: CMOs take over new responsibilities

DOWN: CMOs lose influence within the organization

OUT: CMOs leave the organization

A similar, lateral move is CMOs keeping their job titles but taking over new responsibilities, such as customer service or e-commerce. A prime example would be Airbnb's former CMO, Jonathan Mildenhall, who sought to leverage technology to give a whole new meaning to experiential marketing while simultaneously transforming Airbnb from a tech company to a full-fledged travel brand.

The two other possible trajectories are less savory. First, within their company, CMOs can begin to lose influence with the aforementioned rise of the new C-suite executives, with fewer responsibilities and less opportunity to make real change within the organization. Then, there is the possibility that the company no longer leaves space for a CMO within the organizational structure at all. Coca-Cola recently went this route, eliminating the position altogether in favor of a Chief Growth Officer. According to Forrester Research,[5] some 30 percent of CEOs might fire their CMO in 2017 for lacking the skills necessary to pull off digital business transformation. CMOs are first in the firing line if business growth targets are not met (followed closely by Chief Sales Officers and Chief Strategy Officers), an Accenture Strategy study[6] found.

FIGHT THE COMPETITION: ADOPT A START-UP FRAME OF MIND

To directly address digital disruption and competition, CMOs must adapt both their role and that of their team so that they are set up to innovate in a way that adds tangible value. This evolution can come in a myriad of ways. First off, re-programming the legacy mentality and the CMO role both require returning to a start-up state of mind, no matter how long your company has successfully been in business.

"One of the most important things to remember as a market leader is that we must continually challenge the status quo. Even if we are ahead of our competitors at a point in time, we know that something else is going to happen, and we know that a change is going to come from someone else challenging the business model, challenging the technology base, or whatever else," says David Roman, Chief Marketing Officer of Lenovo. *"We would rather be the challenger, and so we really never take that leader mindset of saying, 'Okay, now we can, in some respect, control the businesses market.' We assume that we can't. We have to continue to challenge ourselves and so I think the challenger mindset is crucial to survival. The challenger mindset is the only thing that will keep you in business."*

INVEST IN INCUBATORS AND NEW PLATFORMS

Another way to tap into this start-up attitude is to look for different types of incubators and partners that will drive innovation and allow the parent company to learn and absorb through proximity and experience. Coca-Cola is building new capabilities by reaching out to those more digitally capable. *"We are smart enough to know what we don't and take the opportunity to learn from partners and start-ups. Coca-Cola was a founding member of an incubator called The Bridge, which essentially looked to help the best and brightest start-ups in Tel Aviv shorten their*

maturity curves and build products and services that could be consumed by large scale CPGs (consumer packaged goods) and beyond," says Francisco Crespo of Coca-Cola. *"Since inception, we have expanded locations across North America, Latin America, and Asia-Pacific, successfully graduating dozens of companies annually. In addition, we constantly are challenging our large scale media, technology, and content partners with pilots to help us fail fast, but learn quickly."*

Mars has also recently created an innovation lab through a collaboration initiative called Launchpad. Mars CMO Andrew Clarke explains that the initiative encourages each local market to pitch ideas focused around the demand challenges that they need to solve using data and technology. Then working with Mediacom and Segment CMOs, Mars looks at all of those briefs and picks the best ones. Three times a year, they will pick around ten at a time, and then look to partner them up with a start-up business externally. Clarke explains:

The objective of this really is twofold. One, I think it is a great way to incubate and experiment with new ideas that we've probably not thought of before…. The second reason for doing it, frankly, is to really help to bring some external talent into Mars so that the digital IQ we can get from start-ups helps to educate and upskill our own associates in our local markets and vice versa. What we can offer start-ups really is the scale and the ability to bring our expertise around big brands—how we reach consumers at scale very quickly. If we can get those partnerships to really work, then there's a real mutual benefit in it for us as we learn and upscale our teams in digital as well as potentially start-ups getting access to our capabilities. That's very, very exciting.

To get to the right people, other brands have focused on loyalty programs, shaping their brand so that it reacts and is exclusive to customers who keep coming back. Maryam Banikarim of Hyatt Hotels says her company wanted to reimagine the loyalty program, but also wanted to discover experiences that would help differentiate Hyatt from the rest of the pack. *"Hyatt is not about size for the sake of size. We're about growing with focus to super-serve the high end of the market and the places that matter most to our targeted guests,"* says Banikarim. *"We leverage the advantages that come from being smaller than our larger competitors yet bigger than the boutiques. We want to use our size and scale to quickly respond to the changing marketplace, knowing our customers better than our competition, and over-performing in each of the segments we're in."* She continues:

In addition to maximizing core business, our strategy is to build, partner, or buy in the areas such as wellness, food and beverage, and alternative accommodations to expand our brand across more dimensions of our travelers' lives. After doing a good deal of analysis we decided to enter the wellness market. Consumers are increasingly looking for ways to be well when at home and on the road and we identified white space in the mindfulness category that we thought presented us with an opportunity. Consumers told us they wanted us to move in this space, but we recognized the need to enter the category with brands that brought an inherent wellness expertise. In 2017, we acquired Miraval, the renowned provider of wellness and mindfulness experiences, and Exhale, the well-being brand that addresses mind and body through spa and fitness. Miraval and Exhale's unique, mindful-centered philosophies are what drew us to those acquisitions.

INVEST IN NEW TECHNOLOGIES

In addition to learning from new acquisitions and incubators, it is also important for companies to invest directly and thoughtfully into technology. GE has done a particularly good job transforming itself from an industrial company into a digital industrial company. As was mentioned in the previous chapter, five or six years ago, the company dove into their strategy to make software the center and brought on all kinds of data entrepreneurs and data scientists to really build out a full value proposition for industrial companies that are trying to monitor their assets remotely—an industrial platform called Predix. To communicate this new advancement, GE launched the Owen campaign, which brought a human and humorous face to a very real technological advancement for GE. *"From a marketing point of view, what we try to do is find ways to bring that new ethos to life,"* says Linda Boff of GE, *"in terms of what we say, where we say it, and how we say it."* It also merged interaction and engagement with technology, as GE has experimented with and organically embraced new platforms into its marketing system as they emerge, like Snapchat, Instagram, Periscope, and other social technologies. While new social tech does not work for every project or company, finding out how to build social into a company identity helps it to reach out to and communicate with a broader and more engaged audience.

In the financial sector, Bank of America is also leading the charge on how financial institutions need to rethink the way they do business. By the end of 2017, Early Warning, in collaboration with major banks like Bank of America, is set to have a large percentage of US banks on the Zelle platform, enabling users to send and receive money across all different financial institutions. This is their answer to other peer-to-peer (P2P) platforms, but with the added support of a trusted bank holding the reins. *"This was our way of saying, 'Listen. We know this is what the millennial population wants,'"* says Meredith Verdone of Bank of America. *"Millennials have been on other P2P platforms and we need to build a better mousetrap and [Zelle] is a better mousetrap in the sense it's more secure, it's free, and it's simpler to use."*

"The difference is that we've got the size and the scale," she continues. *"We bank 16 million millennials, so we've got this tremendous scale and an ability to deepen with them. What's fascinating—and this shocks people—is that millennials still come into financial institutions. They do! They still want to talk to humans, when it's that moment that matters."*

In 2015, Burger King invested in bringing together a group of engineers in-house to form their digital team, based out of New York, which drives the front of technology innovation in their organization. *"Their main goal is to connect the front of house with the back of house to improve the guest experience. Self-order kiosks are one of their priorities. Our mobile order and pay app is something they've been developing, and we're actually testing it in our Miami market now,"* says Axel Schwan of Burger King. *"It's also important for us to consider how all of these things connect to our POS [point of sales]. We want our front of house to connect to the back of house in a way that delivers a seamless experience for our guests."*

KNOW THE CUSTOMER

In order to survive in the age of digital disruption, CMOs need to gear their digital transformation efforts toward developing ways to effectively engage customers through traditional channels and meet their rising expectations. Customer centricity is recognized as one of the main precursors to success. Looking to customers for insight and understanding how to best employ technologies to meet those expectations will help companies relate to consumers whose expectations have indelibly been changed by services like Amazon, Airbnb, and Uber. The consumer market requires engagement and an "always on" experience.

"Consumers are dictating how, when, and why they choose to purchase and consume a beverage, and that is requiring us to rethink our approaches to engagement and the experiences we create to engender loyalty," says Francisco Crespo of Coca Cola. *"We think these disruptions are helping to fuel new innovations and business opportunities for CPGs that didn't exist ten years ago, which result in value for both consumers and customers."*

This requires the effective utilization of technology that is with the consumer throughout their entire purchasing journey. It also requires the adaptation of an "outside-in" approach that allows you to see what is happening in the outside world of data and bringing it into the strategies and projects being worked on internally, as opposed to dictating to the outside world what you think they should be doing and thinking. *"No CMO will ever tell you their budget is big enough,"* says Linda Boff of GE. *"But to me, it's really not about money. It's about figuring out the places to strategically have an impact with the right people."*

CASE STUDY

Coca-Cola TASTE THE FEELING

1 **BACKGROUND:** Marking a significant shift in its marketing strategy, in mid-2016 Coca-Cola announced that for the first time, all of the Coca-Cola brands will be united in one global creative campaign: "Taste the Feeling." This new brand platform replaced "Open Happiness," which launched in 2009. The ads are all based around one core message, "The simple pleasure of drinking any Coca-Cola makes the moment more special." The initial campaign included TV spots, more than 100 campaign images, a new song developed by Avicii, and interactive digital advertising, and was rolled out in regional markets by local agency teams throughout 2016 with localized content under the "Taste The Feeling" umbrella.

2 **PROCESS:** An international network of agencies developed the initial "Taste the Feeling" work. Four agencies—Mercado-McCann, Santo, Sra. Rushmore and Oglivy & Mather—produced an initial round of ten TV commercials, digital, print, out-of-home, and shopper materials with six additional shops contributing to creative as the campaign evolved. Coca-Cola's Chief Marketing Officer at the time, Marcos de Quinto, who unveiled the "one brand" approach at a media event in Paris, asserted that the campaign underscores the company's commitment to choice, offering consumers whichever Coca-Cola suits their taste, lifestyle and diet—with or without calories, with or without caffeine. The shift also represented a change in the overall business approach, with an increase in investment to market all Coca-Cola trademark products across the portfolio under one creative platform.

3 **RESULTS:** In late 2016, Coca-Cola reported that early data coming in from the "Taste the Feeling" launch signaled "green shoots" for their one brand strategy. Coca-Cola's President and COO said, "The early signs from the data are starting to look very encouraging, especially in those places where we launched first and we launched the fastest and the hardest. And we see encouraging results in terms of retail sales growth of the Coca-Cola brand in total." For the Olympic games in Brazil in 2016, Coca-Cola reached 20 million people every day, and their creative focused on "the incredible taste that we feel whenever we overcome, or whenever we win." The result was a dramatic increase in brand feelings among their key teens target, driving their market share up by 1.5 percent and making Coca-Cola the most-associated brand with the Olympics.

KNOW WHAT YOU'RE TALKING ABOUT

While it's not possible for one CMO to know everything about everything, it is important for the CMO to know enough to ask the right questions. This helps interactions with the technology department, and to hire the right people.

A recent survey by Rocket Fuel and Forrester showed marketers are already embracing digital channels and marketing technology.[7] However, the rapid expansion of marketing tools has created a greater need for analysts and data scientists. One in five respondents said a lack of analysts to manage emerging technology was a key barrier to adoption for multi-channel attribution, cross-device delivery and tracking, and data management platforms. To overcome this obstacle, it's important for CMOs to be much more collaborative—to act more as network orchestrators than command-and-control executives.

Bringing in external resources (or leveraging internal ones) to help educate both leadership and the team on best practices is a key way to help transition both the role of the CMO and assist in the transformation of the company. The types of external resources marketing leaders are expected to turn to in the future aren't necessarily the same traditional agency partners they've relied on in the past. The aforementioned Forrester study revealed that technology vendors will have a larger role to play.

Digital transformation is an ongoing process that takes time, training, and effort. CMOs who face the external and internal competition head on have a much greater chance at success than those who don't play a proactive role in jumpstarting their organization's transformation journey.

FIGURE 9

WHAT TYPES of business partners are currently helping you implement predictive capabilities? / What types of business partners do you expect to turn to for implementing predictive marketing capabilities in your organization?"

Currently helping   Expect to help

Our enterprise marketing software vendor
- 39%
- 44%

A technology platform specialized in artficial intelligence
- 34%
- 43%

THE E-COMMERCE REVOLUTION

Over the past several years, e-commerce has proven to be the fastest growing sector in a massive shift toward integrating technology into both business and marketing strategies. According to a report by eMarketer, retail e-commerce sales worldwide rose to $2.290 trillion in 2017,[1] accounting for one-tenth of the total retail sales worldwide. It's only set to grow from there, as new start-ups continue to enter the market and well-established brick and mortar brands aggressively take over large pieces of the e-commerce market.

According to an IRI report, large CPGs alone have lost more than $20 billion to midsize and smaller competitors since 2011.[2] These smaller players are making headway through several channels. Some are finding niche products and untapped consumer segments, while others operate with a start-up mentality, adopting the latest technology and taking risks that larger companies wouldn't typically take. Brands aside from CPGs are also beginning to develop strategies to move into the e-commerce field, setting off a huge race online that changes not only the way consumers shop, but the way marketing teams work as well.

FIGURE 10

MARKET SHARE BY COMPANY SIZE

								2011-15 CAGR	2016 vs. YA
	$606B$			669B$		681B		20.5%	1.7%
Extra Small	8.9%	+1.0		9.9%	+0.4	10.3%		5.3%	5.4%
Small	14.0%	+1.2		15.1%	+0.2	15.3%		4.6%	2.8%
Midsize	19.9%	+0.4		20.3%	+0.0	20.3%		3.1%	1.5%
		(2.6)			(0.5)				
Large	57.2%			54.6%		54.1%		1.3%	0.8%
	2011			**2015**		**2016**			

BEYOND CPG, E-COMMERCE IS EVERYWHERE

Set off and transformed by companies like Amazon, e-commerce has clearly evolved, and now not only demands that CPG brands get their piece of the pie, but forces other industries to respond to the consumer's new need for experiences, intimate service, and instant gratification. Companies can no longer simply approach e-commerce as a separate entity within their organizations. The business model itself must be shifted, and e-commerce needs to be made an integral part of the marketing and sales strategies to differentiate a company of the future with a company that might no longer have one.

"I consider [disruption] as more of an opportunity—particularly in e-commerce," says Theresa Agnew of GSK Consumer Healthcare. She explains:

New brands are always popping up that are competitors, and we need to be present where there is growth. New channels could be seen as disruptors, and we look at them as opportunities. The channel of e-commerce is a growing one in CPG, and especially in consumer healthcare. We're putting a lot of focus and attention there, whether that be through Amazon or Jet or Walmart.com, Target.com, or Walgreens.com, et cetera. We see these partners as great opportunities for growth and joint value creation.

Peter Nowlan of Four Seasons Hotels and Resorts says that, aside from CPG, he sees travel industries and the finance industries as those most disrupted by this drive to digital and e-commerce platforms due to consumer choice, overlap, and the fact that people care deeply about the experience they are planning. *"Travel is among the most disrupted and competitive categories. Never mind brands, whole categories of competitors are emerging. What the consumer wants has changed so much, and I don't think there is a category with as much choice as travel. It's a giant matrix of choices, and I think that is why technology disruption has been so impactful,"* says Nowlan. *"When consumers are booking even just a week-long vacation, they spend at least 30 hours researching in advance. We know that when they book with Four Seasons, 90 percent of the time, they've spent time on our website first, but they've also been to eight or ten other websites."*

Even the financial industry is working to understand how the e-commerce boon requires them to change and evolve in the future, as the habits of their base continue to move toward virtual transactions. *"We're deeply studying the customer and understand their life and making sure we're building for their life, which has given us a lot of impetus to design things very, very differently in order to anticipate,"* says Meredith Verdone of Bank of America.

The lines between online and offline have become increasingly blurry, as is evident by the growing importance of omni-channel marketing strategies that create a seamless customer experience across all channels. One result of this growing trend is that established global brands are facing disruption from several directions as the crowded online ecosystem spills over into brick and mortar sales, and major online retailers seek to expand their offerings. *"Our strategy has definitely evolved where we take more of an omni-channel approach,"* says Theresa Agnew of GSK Consumer Healthcare. *"It's important to understand how the consumer holistically interacts with our categories and brands, and what is happening online that drives to offline and vice versa. Also, our whole approach to what we call a 'digital shelf' has changed. We look at it as we have our retail shelf in bricks and mortar and then we also have our digital shelf."* She continues:

We have to make sure we have the right keywords and terms and the right search strategy for our brands — whether it comes through [a] Google search or through [an] Amazon search. We made a lot of changes in how we do content through our e-commerce partners to make it more SEO optimized. Even just changing the term on a description helps your search quality significantly. We've been able to grow in that space just by making, I think, some simple changes to our digital shelf.

CHANGING BUSINESS MODELS AND MODELS FOR E-COMMERCE

There are many challenges facing today's global brands as they integrate e-commerce into their business strategies. The growing trend in the shift from brick and mortar to digital retail has affected businesses across many sectors. For example, Toys-R-Us announced bankruptcy in early 2017, and a record number of physical retail stores closed their doors in 2017.[3] Consumers in the US are moving from brick and mortar to digital retail with astonishing speed, forcing many traditional retailers to dramatically change the way they approach making sales.

"This encompasses getting the digital foundations and our data set right all the way through to the how we make the decisions with data through our operations...so most significant for us is how this works its way through into digital demands," says Andrew Clarke of Mars. *"How do we reach consumers in new and different ways? How do we convert transactions in new and different ways? How do we add more value in new and different ways, including new business models?"*

Companies in the midst of changing from a primarily brick and mortar retail strategy to an e-commerce based strategy face several challenges, ranging from how to reorganize distribution and supply chain logistics to dealing with more demanding consumer expectations and managing the full-scale digital transformation of sales and marketing. What type of challenges each brand faces, and how they face them, depends on their sector and where they fall on the E-Commerce Digital Growth Matrix.

FIGURE 11

THE E-COMMERCE DIGITAL GROWTH MATRIX

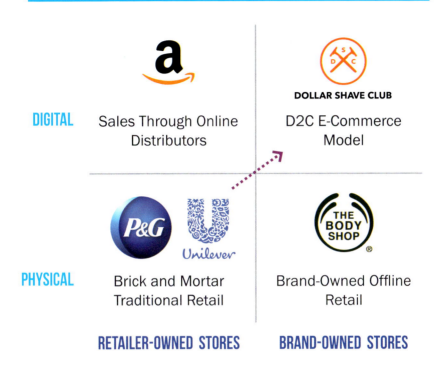

The bottom left corner of this matrix is where big companies—including CPG giants P&G, Nestle, and Unilever—are currently making around 95 percent of their revenue. In this model, not only do the companies gather little to no consumer data from a purchase, they also have no control over the consumer experience. In this age of digital transformation, the consumer journey is not only invaluable to ensuring a conversion, but it also plays a major part in branding and consumer loyalty.

 In the bottom left quadrant are the companies with their own branded physical retail stores, allowing for more control over the consumer experience but still lacking in data. The top left quadrant, which includes retailers like Amazon, Taobao, and Flipkart, is where the online distribution giants have made their home. For many brands, what started out as a symbiotic relationship, where they could use the distribution power behind these online distributors to drive sales, might be working against them now. Essentially what is happening is these brands are paying online retailers to give them aggregate data on their own consumers, but online retailers can leverage that data to take market share away from the very brands they are carrying.

Moving into the top right section of the graph are the companies that have embraced the direct-to-consumer (D2C) model with full control over their own data and customer journey, embodied here by Unilever's Dollar Shave Club. Juliana Chugg of Mattel also reveals why this model works for their American Girl doll:

From a brand perspective, American Girl is a direct-to-consumer business with brick and mortar retail and e-commerce. Forty percent of revenue is generated from e-commerce and is growing as a percentage of the mix as consumers shift to online shopping. This direct relationship with our consumer enables us to understand their buying behavior, the depth of attachment to our brand, and provides us with clear segmentation and micro targeting opportunities.

This is the ideal online setup for many organizations; however, shifting to the D2C model does not come without its own challenges, particularly for CPGs in the food and beverage sector that have to factor in complicated supply chain logistics into their business models. In the case that D2C doesn't make sense for an organization, brands should seek to deepen their relationships with their more established online platforms, like Amazon, Taobao (in China), and Jingdong. Platforms like these are constantly innovating, and brands should keep their packaging, products, and even their supply chain fluidly in line with those of the retailer.

Closer partnerships with these platforms also help brands keep in touch with consumer habits in wildly different markets. For example, the purchasing habits of the Chinese consumer are very different from those in the US, which makes integration difficult. By partnering with people already on the ground, you can employ their expertise to drive purchases.

CASE STUDY

MATTEL PARTNERS WITH ALIBABA FOR GROWTH IN CHINA

1

BACKGROUND: Mattel's goal was to increase their market share through e-commerce in China, one of the largest toy markets in the world. China has approximately 210 million children to the United States' 55 million children—so the market has massive potential. To tap into this market with the right platform and insights to reach Chinese parents, in early 2017, Mattel announced a partnership with China's largest e-commerce player, Alibaba. The agreement will help Alibaba to more aggressively sell Mattel's successful brands like Fisher-Price and Barbie to Chinese consumers to almost 450 million active users, while the toy giant will use the data and consumer insights from Alibaba to develop new toys made specifically for the Chinese market.

2

PROCESS: One big cultural barrier that Mattel and Alibaba will be trying to overcome going forward is that when parents do have extra money to spend on their kids, they try to spend it on educational pursuits for their kids. In response, Mattel wants to develop educational content that will hopefully persuade parents in China that buying toys can have educational benefits too. The toy manufacturer will be working with Alibaba's A.I. Lab to develop innovative educational products, designed to aid the development of children's IQ and EQ through the use of smart, interactive learning and cutting-edge technology. The new, digitally connected toys will be launched in fall 2018.

3

RESULTS: Margo Georgiadis, CEO of Mattel said, "Play has a tremendous impact on a child's cognitive, social, and emotional growth. By combining Mattel's unmatched expertise in childhood learning and development with Alibaba's immense reach and unique consumer insights, our goal is to help parents in China raise children to be their personal best." Mattel's second joint venture in China with Fosun Group aims to really ramp up their educational toy production. One example is Mattel's Hotwheels Speedometry, which are play-based lessons that teach children about subjects such as distance, measurement, potential and kinetic energy, all through building miniature race tracks. As consumers all over the world move away from brick and mortar sales in favor of making purchases online, Mattel is making the effort to be where the consumers are, with the products that they want to buy.

FINDING THE RIGHT TOUCH POINTS

In order to make e-commerce work, brands need to make sure they are interfacing with the consumer at all the right touch points to ensure that the larger digital strategy and e-commerce strategy are the same thing.

According to YH Lee of Samsung, the biggest change to the customer journey is that customers rely on technology more than ever, and there are more brands vying for customer attention, engagement, and loyalty. *"This means it is more difficult to accurately predict the customer's buying decision process,"* she says. *"Groups with demographically similar identities can still show a large variation in purchase patterns depending on their individual lifestyle and values."* For example, single millennial women who are active in sharing information online and investing in self-care (who are active in mobile lifestyle) are less sensitive to price and more active in online shopping through mobile than other single consumers. *"Faced with these realities, marketers need to deliver messages that are not only customized to the right audiences in the right places, but also maintain an authentic human and emotional connection,"* Lee continues.

Purchasing has become an increasingly complicated behavior across diversified channels and platforms. For example, 80 percent of smartphone shoppers[4] use their mobile phone to assist making in-store purchases, but consumers still think of shopping as one experience, regardless of the channel. Brands also need to embrace that mindset—treating the consumer journey as one smooth process, rather than breaking it down into the traditional silos. In order to do this successfully, brands need to do two things: properly leverage their consumer data and develop an omni-channel strategy. They also need to ensure that an e-commerce strategy stays true to the brand voice. *"We have to make sure that every experience we create, every touchpoint we build is authentic to who we are as a brand. A brand that fails to keep its authenticity loses its connections to its consumers,"* says Andres Kiger of Converse. *"Can we keep our brand relevant? Can we make sure that relevancy can drive the business forward?"*

SCALE VERSUS PERSONALIZATION IN THE DIGITAL AGE

Consumer demographics are changing around the globe. Several countries are undergoing a huge middle class expansion—like China and Brazil—while others are facing a rapidly aging population whose purchasing habits are driven by completely different factors than previous generations. Then, of course, there is the new generation of millennials currently rising to power who are digitally savvy and demand more from brands in terms of both shopping experience and quality of product. In short, their purchasing habits are completely different from generations past, and companies are having to quickly adapt their strategies. Now that the consumer journey is no longer black and white, e-commerce can play a significant role outside from simply making purchases. The rise of O2O (online-to-offline) trends has seen companies leverage digital touchpoints to drive people into brick and mortar stores or use gamification in physical retail spaces to add a digital aspect to making purchases. These types of experiences can help drive brand loyalty.

From a marketing standpoint, it might be easy to make the assumption that large global brands have a major advantage over local brands in the form of budget and a global partnerships network. In some cases, it is true that the sheer size of a company's marketing budget might help their message reach more consumers, but in this day and age, that message may be falling on deaf ears if it doesn't come to the right person in the right stage of the consumer journey.

With the level of personalization in marketing that today's consumers have come to expect, the scale of traditional global marketers might not be the competitive advantage that it used to be. It can be very difficult to leverage the right data and successfully execute customization at scale, and in some markets the return on investment (ROI) just isn't there. Many large organizations still operate in traditional silos, and necessary data isn't being shared across teams. Without the right data to leverage, creating a scalable, customized consumer journey can be impossible. However, it is important to note that each industry is different, and this might not be a problem for each marketing team. For example Juliana Chugg of Mattel asserted, *"I think when you go from physical to digital you can provide customization, and you don't need scale because it's digital."*

GLOBAL E-COMMERCE STRATEGIES IN LOCAL MARKETS

The global e-commerce ecosystem is complicated and difficult to map. Each country and region has vastly different consumer profiles, major e-commerce platforms, and online retailers. While Amazon dominates the United States, in China the big players are Taobao and JD, and in India the market is dominated by Flipkart and Snapdeal. This kind of fragmentation presents a unique set of challenges to CMOs pursuing a global e-commerce strategy. It is difficult to align e-commerce strategies in radically different markets all over the globe, and CMOs will need to utilize the strengths of the local markets to ensure that overall global strategy is successful there.

FIGURE 12

TOP TEN COUNTRIES SHARE OF GLOBAL B2C E-COMMERCE MARKET

SHARE OF GLOBAL B2C ECOMMERCE MARKET

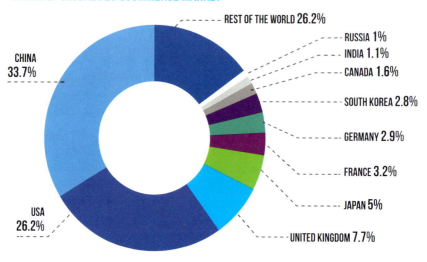

- REST OF THE WORLD **26.2**%
- RUSSIA **1**%
- INDIA **1.1**%
- CANADA **1.6**%
- SOUTH KOREA **2.8**%
- GERMANY **2.9**%
- FRANCE **3.2**%
- JAPAN **5**%
- UNITED KINGDOM **7.7**%
- USA **26.2**%
- CHINA **33.7**%

"The challenge for us is how [can] we get that balance right between global and local? While it's not always easy, I think today that presents lots of opportunities as well," says Andrew Clarke of Mars. *"How do we use brilliant global platforms for our brands, enabling local markets to innovate with the creative locally to reach consumers in new ways? How do we use the appropriate technology where we can scale across geographies? How do we use data? How do we use partnerships and relationships? How do we have a higher order test and learn agenda on behalf of the business?"*

"Marketing's role is not just about branding. It's about the brand, driving the business, and building platforms for sustainable competitive advantage."

RAJA RAJAMANNAR
Mastercard

In order to really target consumers, Clarke and his team worked on ways to utilize their big global brand platforms and ways to bring the products to a local network in new and innovative ways. He explains:

We're using our local teams, our agencies in the markets. We can do things using tech and data and digital in very new and different ways. Snickers is a great example. The global platform of 'You're Not You When You're Hungry' is now in over 70 countries. Snickers Hungerithm, as an example, started in Australia in a partnership with 7-Eleven and Snickers. We did a pretty innovative thing there where the team there was actually using the mood of the internet. When it got angrier, the price of Snickers came down using data and algorithms, and that led to coupons being available for consumers to then take into a 7-Eleven to buy cheaper Snickers. That got a lot of media attention. A really good example of taking a global positioning but innovating locally and executing locally. I would argue that if we get this right, this gives us a competitive advantage, but of course it's very, very challenging as things move quickly.

FIGURE 13

THE RISE OF THE SUPERCONSUMER

A recent survey of online shoppers revealed that for the first time they bought more of their purchases online rather than in stores.

How purchases are made

Share of purchases made online

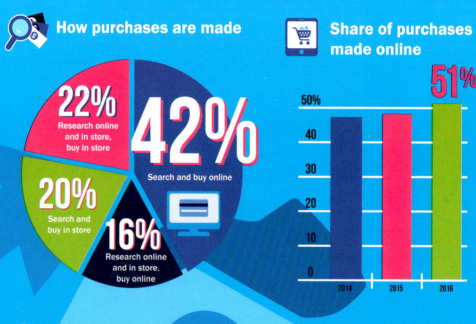

22% Research online and in store, buy in store

20% Search and buy in store

42% Search and buy online

16% Research online and in store, buy online

51%

50%
40
30
20
10
0

2014   2015   2016

Purchasing on a smartphone by generation

MILLENNIALS	**63%**
GEN XERS	**41%**
BABY BOOMERS	**19%**
SENIORS	**8%**

THE RISE OF THE SUPERCONSUMER

According to a study by eMarketer, e-commerce sales growth will stay in the double digits yearly until 2021,[5] with retail e-commerce sales worldwide increasing at four times the rate of retail sales this year, jumping 23.2 percent to $2.290 trillion. In 2017, mobile commerce alone will account for more than 70 percent of e-commerce sales in both China and India, and 59 percent in South Korea. In Germany, the UK, and US, mobile commerce (m-commerce) will comprise at least one-third of total retail e-commerce sales.

At this point, nearly every industry—from early adopters in the hospitality and tourism sector to newcomers like luxury retailers—have adopted some type of e-commerce strategy to capture a slice of this lucrative pie. Their strategies have to shift with the trends in e-commerce and the rise of the so-called "superconsumer." Global consumers have shifted toward leading truly mobile lives, and a significant amount of consumers are making more purchases online than in stores. Purchasing habits have also been subject to cultural shifts, as millennials have more and more buying power. "*We need to stay attuned to ensure we have the right offerings from our brands for the changing needs of our consumers,*" says Theresa Agnew of GSK Consumer Healthcare. "*In consumer healthcare, we are focused not just on treatment solutions but also on wellness. How we approach that is really critical. There is an evolving trend especially with millennial consumers around wanting more natural products and wellness solutions. We take a holistic health and wellness approach as we look at our innovation and our services.*"

In addition, the share of global internet traffic taken up by mobile phones is up 30 percent over last year, according to a recent We Are Social report.[6] This means the number of digital touchpoints available for brands to connect with consumers and make conversions is growing every year, and being present online is now critical for a brand's success. Truly serious consumer-centric brands, no matter the industry, need to embrace e-commerce going forward or risk continuing to lose market share to companies with agile, fast-moving digital strategies.

There is also the next phase of "Amazonification." While the e-commerce side has already changed the logistics of consumers buying goods, brands are also putting greater emphasis on integrating the power of social media with commerce. Think more customer reviews and product information integrated with the shopping experience, and people using their own social network to influence purchasing decisions. Social commerce is already here with brands able to sell directly to consumers on platforms like Instagram and Facebook, and it is a huge trend in Asian markets—China in particular—on platforms like WeChat.

USE TECHNOLOGY TO DIFFERENTIATE

The leading companies of the future will also be leaders in technology. These innovators will be tapping into the needs of consumers who are looking for new experiences that are both novel but also help them to accomplish what they want. For Bank of America, this meant doing a deep dive to research what was going on in other markets, especially with China and the WeChat pay phenomenon. *"One thing is to anticipate the future: not what a bank is going to look like but how is a customer going to live their life,"* says Meredith Verdone of Bank of America. *"[When you look at it this way], what do they need, which is a really different question to ask."*

Differentiating also means taking some risks in new technologies that may still be considered a bit fringe but can be incredibly useful for certain industries. Technologies like augmented reality and virtual reality can actually energize an e-commerce platform. Nowhere is this more obvious than some of the campaigns coming out of China. Take, for instance, the big player Yihaodian. Using augmented reality, the massive online grocery platform opened virtual stores around China in public parks, tourist spaces, and even parking lots. Customers with the app could use the mobile platform to wander the "aisles" and touch products on the screen to add them to the cart. Mattel's Juliana Chugg reveals how the toy giant is integrating these cutting-edge technologies into their traditional product:

Take, for example, American Girl; our last edition of our catalog was the wish book for the holidays where we introduced augmented reality. This enabled brand fans to unlock content and bring character narratives to life when [they] took [their] device, either a phone or iPad, and scanned it over the images on the page unlocking engaging content that enhanced the user experience. Leveraging technology to create high levels of engagement in building brand affinity is a key area of focus to keep our brands relevant to today's technologically savvy consumers.

Andres Kiger of Converse touches on their inspiration in the e-commerce space, including smaller disruptors making strides in the market:

These days, it is increasingly important to keep our eyes wide open and seek inspiration from everywhere. These days, 'disruptive genius' does not only come from big and global brands. Smaller and local brands are doing great work, showing how to keep the spirit of innovation alive and how to do a lot with fewer resources. It's also interesting to see how they actually design and manage to build new brand connections. Global brands are quickly learning that the playing field is leveling and that big and small brands can provide to be formidable competitors.

The most important aspect of any company's e-commerce strategy is proving that the efforts of the marketing team link to significant business results. The traditional role of the marketing function has always been to build brand health, but in today's world, it is easier to track how that brand health translates into a transaction. Mukul Deoras of Colgate-Palmolive explains:

I need to build and measure the health of a brand, and then the demand will get generated. That link remains the same. But now, there is a direct way of actually shifting the health of a brand into a transaction. Marketers now have a more direct contribution toward revenue generation than they've ever had, particularly in the e-commerce sector. For example, our China business is one of our largest e-commerce businesses, and our Hill's Pet nutrition business is also a very large e-commerce business. It is absolutely possible for marketing to see where they have contributed to revenue.

The role of marketing has evolved beyond getting messages out to consumers, and now the function has the real power to affect change and bring in real ROI. Mastercard's Raja Rajamannar agrees, saying, *"Marketing's role is not just about branding. It's about the brand, driving the business, and building platforms for sustainable competitive advantage."*

LEVERAGING BIG DATA

A BLESSING AND A CURSE

Of the many marketing tools CMOs need to have under their belts during this shift from traditional to digital channels, big data and analytics is one of the most important, and the most challenging to get right. Today, a fundamental component of how a company benchmarks its customer centricity is through its data and analytics strategy. Companies are also in the midst of a data-rich boon. Fueled by mobile data, e-commerce, and the rise of consumer-focused products and strategies, the digital age is also creating a huge stash of information about consumers, giving companies unprecedented insights into the behavior of their consumers.

"Data is a big enabler in understanding consumer behavior," says Francisco Crespo of Coca-Cola. *"Not only the change but also the differential in behavior between offline and online. Machine learning is opening new possibilities on how data can be mined for core insights."*

Customer centricity strategies not only leverage data to provide highly relevant experiences, but they also generate relevant new data and use technology to make real-time personalized customer decisions where possible. The growth of Internet of Things (IoT), which is a connected network of physical devices, from home appliances to vehicles and wearable electronics, that can connect and exchange data via the internet, as well as the increasingly digital consumer journey means that the amount of data at the fingertips of marketers is only set to increase in the coming years. Gartner, Inc.[1] says that 8.4 billion connected things were in use worldwide in 2017 and will reach 20.4 billion by 2020, which means that, even more than today, companies are going to be with their consumer every step of the way.

FIGURE 14

THE INTERNET OF THINGS

8.4 BILLION

8.4 BILLION connected things will be in use worldwide in 2017, up 31% from 2016, and will reach 20.4 billion by 2020.

$2 TRILLION

Total spending on endpoints and services will reach almost **$2 TRILLION** in 2017.

67 PERCENT

Greater China, North America and Western Europe together will represent **67%** of the overall IoT installed base in 2017.

$5.2 BILLION

The consumer segment is the largest user of connected things with **5.2 BILLION** units in 2017, which represents 63% of the overall number of applications in use

GE is at the very forefront of IoT technology, building solutions that help other companies on their journey to digitally transform all aspects of their business. *"We have started to really build out a full value proposition for industrial companies that are trying to monitor their assets remotely and manage their assets with greater proficiency. Starting with this business strategy led us to Predix, our industrial IoT platform specifically designed for the unique and complex challenges of industrial data,"* says Linda Boff of GE.

CASE STUDY

THE INDUSTRIAL INTERNET

1 **BACKGROUND:** At GE, their in-house term for the Internet of Things (IoT)—the "Industrial Internet"—is not only helping to drive GE into the future of digital transformation, but they are also helping other organizations transform their businesses to be ready for the digital future. In 2012, GE began development of Predix, a software platform for collecting and analyzing data from industrial machines. In order to test the software, oil and gas giant BP outfitted 650 of its thousands of oil wells with GE sensors as part of a pilot program. Each well was outfitted with anywhere from 20 to 30 sensors to measure factors like temperature and pressure, and they transmitted around 500,000 data points to the Predix cloud every 15 seconds. For GE, Predix will ultimately serve as a standard way to to connect machines, data, and people across multiple industries.

2 **PROCESS:** GE determined that the market for a platform and applications in the industrial segment was enormous—with the potential to reach $225 billion by 2020. After GE's pilot test with BP's oil rig sensors, GE needed to transform the platform to connect, secure, and analyze the data from these massive datasets. Predix can do just that, providing machine operators and maintenance engineers with real-time information to schedule maintenance checks, improve machine efficiency, and reduce downtime. Predix has applications across many industries, and with this solution, GE is helping other companies jump-start their own digital transformations. In 2015, GE launched their "What's the Matter With Owen?" campaign. In the ad Owen tells his parents and friends that he has just landed a computer programming job — with GE. Owen tells them that he will be writing code to help machines communicate, but they're confused because GE isn't a software company.

3 **RESULTS:** The Owen campaign was just part of GE's massive digital transformation efforts that spans across the organization, from their actual technology solutions, all the way across to their marketing and HR functions.

Today, using Predix technology, GE already captures 50 million data points collected and communicated by 10 million sensors installed on over $1 trillion worth of technical equipment, ranging from locomotives to jet engines and medical imaging systems—proving that big data will soon be an integral part of most business strategies in the near future.

However, according to a survey conducted by IBM,[2] a vast majority of CMOs consider themselves unprepared to manage the impact that digital disruption has on their own marketing functions, and the explosion of data at their fingertips is at the top of the list. Data is the foundation that good digital marketing is built upon, but if it's not used correctly, it can also account for confusing leads, false paths, and scattered strategies. In short, the sheer amount of information we now have about consumers is both a blessing and a curse.

FIGURE 15

THE VAST MAJORITY OF CMOS ARE UNDERPREPARED TO MANAGE THE IMPACT OF TOP MARKET FACTORS AFFECTING THE MARKETING FUNCTION

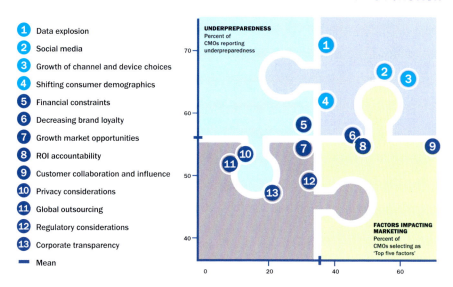

1. Data explosion
2. Social media
3. Growth of channel and device choices
4. Shifting consumer demographics
5. Financial constraints
6. Decreasing brand loyalty
7. Growth market opportunities
8. ROI accountability
9. Customer collaboration and influence
10. Privacy considerations
11. Global outsourcing
12. Regulatory considerations
13. Corporate transparency
— Mean

DRIVE DATA, DON'T LET IT DRIVE YOU

Data can be used in a myriad of ways, but in essence, it is only useful when being leveraged to better and more deeply understand a business. In other words, make the data work for you. As CMOs say again and again, the core of marketing has not changed, merely the vehicles with which to achieve goals have.

"We know data is a key enabler for dissecting consumer behavior. We are not at a loss for data. However, we know that changes are happening at an accelerating pace, and we must be able to aggregate, ingest, and standardize consumer data in real time,"

says Francisco Crespo of Coca-Cola. *"Once we have established the foundation, we know we need to leverage existing and new forms of data science to identify and extract the most powerful insights. This would, in theory, leverage a combination of human and electronic minds to surface most relevant behavioral patterns from which we could make business decisions."*

The key is not to become overwhelmed by the sheer bulk of data at hand. Most organizations are swimming in first party data—data that comes to them directly from the consumer—that can come from marketing automation, social media, mobile apps, customer relationship management (CRM) data, website usage, and several other sources. Then there is third party data streaming in from other sources. One challenge many organizations are having is that data is siloed across an organization, with little to no sharing happening between teams. This means strategies are being built with gaping blind spots, which can prevent the marketing team from having a holistic view of the organization's consumers.

"Data is an important tool to help you better understand your customers and their needs," says Maryam Banikarim of Hyatt Hotels. *"But in the end, it's about what you do with the data. You still need to get in front of your customer and engage them—that hasn't changed. Storytelling is still the most effective communications technique. Today, you just now have a better chance of getting your story to the right person in the right place at the right time...."*

Meredith Verdone of Bank of America highlights the importance of not getting lost in all the data, and leveraging the right type of business savvy talent that will understand how to balance both and data to make the right decisions:

I think you still need smart business people—people with an incredible gut about some of the decisions that we make. People who really understand how you're delivering the brand. Because in all that data, you can get so far down the funnel that you forget what you stand and forget what your brand stands for.

DEFINE A DATA ANALYTICS STRATEGY

For data to do its job, it's important to have a data analytics strategy in place that will clearly improve a predetermined performance. Like e-commerce web-

FIGURE 16

HOW COMPANIES ARE USING BIG DATA

Functional areas where companies do, and should, focus on using big data and analytics to improve overall performance. All data in percentages.

- Customer insights, segmentation, or targeting — IDEALLY 60 / CURRENTLY 49
- Budgeting, forecasting, or planning — IDEALLY 36 / CURRENTLY 39
- Operations, service delivery, or supply chain management — IDEALLY 41 / CURRENTLY 37
- Customer service/support — IDEALLY 40 / CURRENTLY 33
- Performance management and transparency in interal operations — IDEALLY 39 / CURRENTLY 30
- New product strategies — IDEALLY 40 / CURRENTLY 28
- Pricing — IDEALLY 29 / CURRENTLY 21
- Automation of common or straightforward decisions — IDEALLY 18 / CURRENTLY 13
- Improvements to R&D processes — IDEALLY 19 / CURRENTLY 12

● IDEALLY
● CURRENTLY

sites, each company must determine what they will build from the ground up, purchase, borrow, or rent. In some cases, the ability to collect first party data using deep, internal data and analytics expertise is invaluable—but for others, the investment outweighs the benefits. There are long-term third party contracts to consider, or partnerships with customers, suppliers, and other marks along the supply chain. For many companies, it's a combination of the three. But what is all important is finding the right combination that backs up the clear vision you have for the company, and building the system around that.

An initiative called Synapse, developed and run by Andrew Clarke's team from Mars, takes on these big demand challenges that the company has across the segments. Clarke and his team put proper resources, dollars, and partnerships in place to run an extensive demand science test and learn agenda. This helped them to flesh out areas where they had gaps in knowledge, as well as target areas where they could possibly have a competitive advantage in the future. Some of the briefs they worked on were how to conduct more transactions in new and different ways using data and technology, and how to get a better read on ROI for their media dollars in new digital channels. Clarke explains:

Synapse is helping show us how we can use data to understand big data on a macro level, to see clearly some of the trends that are happening with our consumers, and therefore what it means for our portfolio and how we innovate. We are one of the world's leading advertisers. We spend billions of dollars a year on advertising. Being able to prove the effectiveness of our creative much quicker gives us a much better chance to reinvest those dollars in new and different ways to drive growth. The more we can push out our knowledge and understanding, the better we can reinvest our dollars to drive growth and to make our brands relevant.

CUSTOMER-CENTRIC MARKETING TECHNOLOGY

Driving and benchmarking customer centricity through a data and analytics strategy is key in evolving as a business in today's landscape. By focusing the consumer's needs, you not only use consumer data to provide intimate experiences, but you can also generate new data based on their reactions, and eventually use technology to make personalized customer decisions in real time.

Axel Schwan and his team at Burger King use a mix of big data and small data to complement each other and get them closer to their guest. Almost all of their tills in their restaurants around the world are connected to the central system, and the resulting data (which they call their Product Mix) allows them to basically see not only if advertising is working, but also how promotions work. This means they can adjust what they are doing along the way, either to make the campaign stronger or to change plans if it doesn't work. This data is also bundled into the data they work with, which they get off of their digital app and their social listening. Schwan says this really "helps us connect to our guests in new and meaningful ways."

He also cannot drive home enough the importance of so-called "small data." *"When we have new product ideas, technology ideas, advertising ideas, and guest experience ideas that we want to use to change the restaurant environment in some way, we like to observe people,"* says Schwan. *"Real observation is key, in all shapes and forms, because you need to find the story. It's all about the stories, and you need to have the data—big and small—to help you craft the stories in the right way."*

> *"Every large business of course has lots of challenges, lots of new competition that maybe didn't exist five years ago, and lots of challenges with the fragmentation of media. How do we reach consumers in new and different ways within the changing channel mix? That's not new to us, that's new for everyone. We all face that challenge. The question is how do you respond to that challenge with a degree of agility while ensuring your decisions are based in facts?"*

ANDREW CLARKE
Mars

Most industries have adopted a similar consumer-first mindset, using data as the motor to drive these strategies. Theresa Agnew of GSK Consumer Healthcare says:

In my opinion, you need to turn data into knowledge. It's not just about how much data you have, but how you use it and how you make it actionable, which is why we will keep putting our analytics and insights resources together so that we're looking at data holistically. I say that's the big challenge, but it's also the opportunity to do that well.

INTEGRATING BRANDING AND BIG DATA

While data has become a critical tool in deepening consumer insights and allowing for quicker reaction times, it is important not to leave behind classic methods of insight development to guide brand and strategy. This is not to say one should be a replacement for the other, but rather they need to work in tandem; insights gathered from social listening and third party digital data provide a richer and more well-rounded picture that can be used for brand strategy and development. By using search data, you can not only tell how often your brand has been sought out, but also how closely its associated with your brand value proposition based on the click-through rate on keywords.

David Roman of Lenovo likes to say that, in the end, marketing doesn't really change that much in terms of the role within the business. To him, marketing has always been about collecting analytical information, translating that into insights, and then using a creative component in terms of how marketers tell their company's story in a way that is compelling to those being targeted. Roman elaborates:

Although technology is changing constantly and big data is important, the skills of marketing are still the same. You figure out where the most attractive audiences to go after are. How do I tell the story to them? How do I bring it to them? I think the tools keep on evolving, but if you lose sight of that bigger picture, you end up being too focused on one part of the tool. I think some people really convince themselves that with big data, in the end, marketing will be something you throw all that data into and it will spit out the marketing. It doesn't work that way. Everybody has the same data; everybody has the same thing. Maybe you get some advantage in a very, very short time if you move a little bit faster, but it's not going to be a sustainable advantage in the end.

Syl Saller of Diageo agrees, saying that having both the technology knowledge and classic marketing skills are equally important:

Today's marketers must be storytellers who are data lovers—and by this I mean they must have a balance of left-brain and right-brain skills; they must be creative minds who also have demonstrable skills in analytics, customization, personalization, and optimization to drive sophisticated investment decisions. Becoming more digital and data-driven is paramount and represents a massive shift culturally to balance a creative ballast with understanding of effectiveness.

CREATING A SEAMLESS CONSUMER JOURNEY

The true customer journey is the sum of the different experiences customers have over many different channels and touchpoints, both online and offline. Each experience can cause behavior changes that alter the journey in a positive or negative way. Big data allows you to bring together the entire journey (sometimes over many years and transactions) and dig deep into the data to see how each experience interacting with the brand had an impact on the journey. It's important to see all three of these items—touchpoints, experience, and impact—to understand what will drive conversions. However, there are still some black boxes in the modern consumer journey that data won't be able to open but are still key in reaching the end of the purchase funnel. YH Lee of Samsung describes how they are tackling this challenge:

We are currently in the process of developing a unified global data platform integrating Samsung data. We collect consumer engagement signals, such as impressions, clicks, and visits from emails, media ad servers, and Samsung.com, to identify consumer interest in specific products and deliver tailored messages to boost conversion.

FIGURE 17

MODERN PURCHASE PATH

Lee explains further by using a typical consumer journey from Samsung as an example:

Samsung stores allow potential customers to get hands-on experience with our new products, learn from our experts, and directly order products from in-store digital signage and tablets. We also encourage customers to use Samsung.com or our mobile app to purchase online and pick-up from a nearby store. The service is running in key countries, and we will expand this to other markets in the near future. Furthermore, when consumers buy products, they trust the rating and opinions of power bloggers and social influencers more than corporate advertisements and sales messages, so it is essential to utilize these influencers as brand ambassadors (brand advocates).

These are just some of the many ways that consumers interact with Samsung on their way toward making a purchase *"It is important to creatively design the customer journey, including online and offline touch points, that improve the customer experience through these channels,"* Lee adds.

Even with all of this data, many insights might be well-hidden. In the case of the customer journey, you need to see the trees from the forest—find the unique correlations that create the big picture. Leading big data analytics platforms provide advanced analytics and data discovery to find the hidden patterns in the data that make up the journey and, more importantly, are guiding the journey. This may lead to correlations and conclusions you never considered before, such as unknown paths customers are taking and sentiment that customers express along their journey.

"Every large business of course has lots of challenges, lots of new competition that maybe didn't exist five years ago, and lots of challenges with the fragmentation of media," says Andrew Clarke of Mars. *"How do we reach consumers in new and different ways within the changing channel mix? That's not new to us, that's new for everyone. We all face that challenge. The question is how do you respond to that challenge with a degree of agility while ensuring your decisions are based in facts?"*

This is where the strength of a company's belief in evidence-based marketing comes into play. *"There's lots of noise, lots of opinions, lots of perspectives. Every day, there are articles written,"* Clarke continues. *"It's about really stepping back from that and being smart about how we use data to inform our decisions; to amplify and scale up things we know work, but also to be bold and test new things and evaluate their effectiveness."*

BRINGING IN EXTERNAL RESOURCES

In order to take full advantage of the big data revolution, CMOs must be cognizant of expanding their expertise in order to grow the marketing team and truly unlock the full potential of data and analytics. To keep their position and their organization competitive, they'll need to understand the infrastructure that supports, processes, and protects customer data through software. This does not mean the CMO needs to be the ultimate authority on all things data. But they will need to better understand data technology and innovation in order to work closely with the Chief Innovation Officer or Technology Officer and balance parallel business requirements and achieve overarching goals.

Like any new business endeavor, data analytics will not reach its potential without a clear, well-articulated strategy and success benchmarks. Sometimes companies can fall short if no one in the top leadership is charged with working on this, has time to dig into the issue, or lacks the expertise they need. Organizations will need more analytics experts but also someone who can drive the transition with a clear plan that establishes priorities and well-defined pathways toward business results. This new environment requires management skills and leadership that will help the rest of the endeavor thrive.

Frontline activities—like mobilizing resources and building capabilities—will need to take place at the business unit or functional level, for two reasons. First, the priorities for using data analytics to increase revenues and productivity will differ by business. Second, and just as important, companies best catalyze frontline change when they connect it with core operations and management priorities and reinforce it with clear metrics and targets.

"Like all industries, I think the biggest change will be in how we use data to connect with people in a way that suits them and respects their privacy," says Syl Saller of Diageo. *"There will be a massive shift in how we use the ever-increasing abundance of data to sharpen and refine consumer insight and then create the right content in such a way that we are providing either utility, entertainment, or ideally both."*

BLENDING DATA AND CREATIVITY

Data is now crucial to almost every aspect of today's marketing function, but it cannot be integrated at the expense of storytelling and creativity. *"I think this role of what we call data scientists is one which is interesting because we've got a lot of analytically focused people, but I don't think that necessarily makes them data scientists,"* says Meredith Verdone of Bank of America.

She emphasizes that while data is important, understanding why the data looks the way it does is what allows the marketing strategy to be impactful to consumers. Verdone continues:

We're asking people to operate with both the right and the left side of their brain. Neither left-brained people nor right-brained people are people who can fully bring in all the pieces of understanding to the data. It takes understanding the world around us with context, understanding how to communicate, work collaboratively and work in real time. It's a really different skill set that we're asking people to have, and you need much more.

Pizza Hut's David Timm echoes this sentiment, asserting that in moving from a simple to complex marketing model, it is crucial for marketers not to lose sight of the brand message across the data-driven and complex landscape. He says:

We're moving from a very simple marketing model. When I say simple, I don't mean easy. I mean simple but very difficult to do well. Mass marketing, almost by definition, is: you pick an audience, you pick a message, and then you broadcast it as extensively as you can through a combination of reach and frequency. That's a really simple model that is difficult to do well because you have to be distinctive, and you have to be culturally relevant. But, the new world is a more complex one with multiple audiences, multiple messages, real-time execution, data-driven, and fragmented over additional channels. That's the first piece that is going to be very different for marketers—understanding that you're moving from simple to complex. The second piece of it is that you still need to present the brand to your consumers in a coherent manner despite the multiple messages and audiences.

So what type of company will win in this new world? According to Juliana Chugg of Mattel, it will be the ones that leverage the vast swathes of data to provide consumers with what they really want: experiences. She explains:

Companies that will win in the future are the ones that offer differentiated, relevant user experiences. When you think about Uber, they don't own any physical cars, but the user experience is dramatically enhanced relative to the former transportation model. The ease of access, the information that you have as to when your car will arrive, the seamless ability to pay and understand the cost of the experience, and to have your driver rated based on other users experiencing that driver provides enhanced utility that improves your experience. Our focus is on the consumer; to be so consumer-centric and focused on providing differentiated user experiences that increase the attachment rate to our brands in ways that are purposeful and meaningful is what we wake up every day focused on delivering.

CASE STUDY

PIZZA HUT'S APPROACH TO BIG DATA

1 **BACKGROUND:** Big data is finding its place in the digital transformation and marketing strategies of companies across every sector. Since the early 2010s, Pizza Hut has been finding new ways to leverage data across several key markets. Whether it's using digital, interactive menus in-store to capture data about the decision making process of their consumers, partnering with Toyota to change the future of pizza deliveries, or letting customers order pizza through their app by "reading their minds," Pizza Hut is one restaurant testing the limits of what data can do.

2 **PROCESS:** Back in 2014, Pizza Hut developed an app with eye control software vendor, Tobii, that allowed consumers to order pizza with their "minds." The software behind the app tracked consumers eye movements while looking at pictures of ingredients, and whichever ones the eyes lingered on longer were combined by an algorithm into the consumer's perfect "subconscious" pizza. Since then, Pizza Hut has rolled out several big data initiatives in different regions, including the adoption of APT software to analyze pricing, capital investment, promotion, marketing and operations data. This move was to leverage data to garner a deeper understanding of the ROI of every action taken within the organization, where even small changes can affect consumer loyalty. The pizza giant also infused data into their Hong Kong loyalty program, leveraging data taken from users' ordering habits and 3D printing technology to create eight mini versions of its most popular Pizza Hut dishes. For every purchase over a designated amount, Pizza Hut customers received a Mini Plate of the designated dish for free. Each Mini Plate had a QR code linking back to its point-of-sale.

3 **RESULTS:** Pizza Hut's forays into the world of big data have been largely successful, and in early 2018 the chain announced its most ambitious project yet, a partnership with Toyota to begin work on autonomous delivery options. In addition to delivery solutions, the two companies will immediately begin working on initiatives to improve the existing driver/delivery ecosystem through big data. Starting in early 2018, Toyota and Pizza Hut will test dual communication technology in Pizza Hut delivery vehicles that will capture data on driver patterns and behaviors. This data will hopefully result in improved performance for both companies, enhancing delivery operations while also optimizing the safety of delivery. Pizza Hut's other data-driven initiatives include voice-activated ordering with Alexa and the creation of their start-up, Pizza Hut Digital Ventures, meant to modernize the pizza ordering experience all over the world.

TECHNOLOGY AND THE CMO

The technology available to today's marketing teams is expansive, sometimes convoluted, and advancing to new heights every day. From the increasingly fragmented (and growing) landscapes of martech and adtech, to the rise of previously exotic sci-fi technologies like artificial intelligence (AI) and gamification, there are a vast number of tools available at the fingertips of today's CMOs. The questions that remain are: Which of these tools are right for individual situations? How can marketers harness these technologies to advance the entire company's agenda in a sustainable and measurable way?

THE RAPIDLY CHANGING TECHNOLOGY LANDSCAPE

As businesses are moving toward more digital platforms and ideas, so too are the tools being used behind the scenes to help agencies and brands target, deliver, and analyze their marketing and advertising. Traditionally, advertising technology has focused on display, targeting, mobile marketing, and audience monetization via networks and exchanges. It builds the outward brand to attract potential customers and track the effects of marketing activities on revenue. Marketing technology, however, takes a more personable approach, focusing on campaign management, social and email marketing, and lead management—essentially reaching out to customers. Tools and software filed under the marketing technology category use direct methods of fostering good relationships with those who have been identified as a company's target audience (which typically includes past customers or those who have expressed interest in becoming customers).

Today, adtech-driven programmatic and real-time bidding digital media buying strategies have surpassed "traditional" digital advertising, and *Business Insider* says these approaches will represent 50 percent of digital ad sales in 2018.[1] Using martech and adtech software efficiently is critical to ensure that your marketing dollars are working as hard as they can and proving ROI on marketing spends. An industry survey conducted by PwC and sponsored by the Interactive Advertising Bureau (IAB) found that digital ad spending not only surpassed TV in 2016,[2] but in a clear sign of a rapidly maturing channel, mobile surged past the "traditional" digital warhorse of search, accounting for 50.52 percent of all revenue. The first quarter of 2017 also broke boundaries, marking the highest ever first quarter earnings for digital advertising in the United States, hitting $19.6 billion and marking the seventh consecutive first quarter to have double-digit, year-on-year growth.

BLURRED LINES

The adtech/martech landscape itself is a rather jumbled one, chock full of vendors trying to jockey for position in an increasingly fragmented environment. Maps of the different types of technology solutions available to marketers have become a popular way to visualize how intricate this landscape is. First popularized by the Lumascape, a map developed by adtech banker Terry Kawaja in 2010, this visual helped map the rapidly burgeoning adtech/martech ecosystem from marketer to consumer, from agency to programmatic buyer. As the environment has grown and shifted, so too has the Lumascape, expanding every year to capture the growing web of players.

FIGURE 18

INTERNET ADVERTISING QUARTERLY REVENUE GROWTH TRENDS

1996-2016 ($billions)

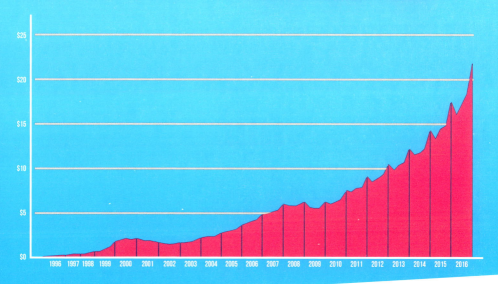

YEARLY REVENUE NUMBERS IN $BILLIONS

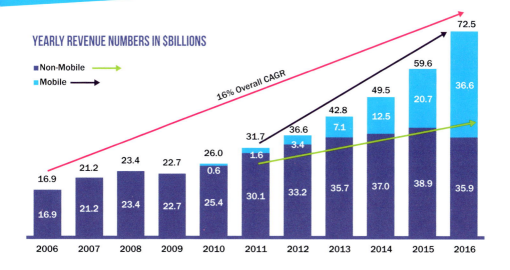

FIGURE 19

THE RAPIDLY EXPANDING TECHNOLOGY LANDSCAPE

The 2017 edition of the martech map developed by
SCOTT BRINKER OF THE **CHIEF MARKETING TECHNOLOGIST BLOG** FEATURES:

5,381 SOLUTIONS

UP 39% YEAR-ON-YEAR

FROM 4891 UNIQUE COMPANIES.

The Lumascape point toward growth in the marketplace, rather than consolidation, with just

4.7% of the solutions removed from the map since the 2016 edition.

ONLY 6.9% are enterprises with more than 1000 employees or a public listing.

NEARLY HALF are investor-funded start-ups at any pre-exit stage (48.8%), and 44.2% are private businesses with **FEWER THAN 1000** staff and no funding data.

In 2011, when the Lumascape was created, it featured about 150 companies, growing to 350 in 2012 and more than 2000 by 2015.

150   300   2000+

As these technologies and software continue to develop and the tech companies themselves are merging, being acquired, or partnering to offer more holistic services, the lines separating adtech and martech continue to blur. In the "new normal" of marketing, where digital is no longer considered new media and is accounting for an increasing percentage of global ad spends every year, technology-driven marketing and advertising campaigns are at the forefront of innovation. Technology can drive marketing approaches starting from the conceptual stage—using data-driven solutions to personalize ads or select a specific target audience—all the way to measuring the key performance indicators (KPIs) using attribution tech solutions. As marketing activities are increasingly breaking out of traditional internal silos, the technologies driving these activities are merging as well.

THE RISE OF PROGRAMMATIC ADVERTISING

Programmatic advertising comprises of the use of software and data to purchase display ads that are targeted toward particular audiences, rather than purchased by channel. This is one of the most significant waves of innovation to ever hit advertising, and the innovation and growth of this sector is unlikely to slow down.

Programmatic buying primarily uses data management platforms (DMPs) and demand side platforms (DSPs), which advertisers and their agencies use to buy display inventory on ad exchanges. DSPs provide centralized media buying from several sources, while DMPs help to centralize cookie data to assist advertisers in creating segments that should be specifically targeted. For example, DMPs target display ads for anti-aging face cream toward those most likely to be worrying about their skin. In turn, publishers (companies who are renting out ad space or placing it) make their inventory available through supply side platforms (SSPs), which provide media selling and network management services for publishers.

This automated media buying model has taken the world by storm in recent years. Google alone has targeted more than 60 percent of its digital marketing budget for programmatic campaigns, which Proctor and Gamble (the world's biggest media spender) aims to buy 50–70 percent of its US digital media programmatically. A significant portion of display ad budgets are also already traded in real time. In the US alone, eMarketer estimated that nearly four of every five digital display dollars will transact programmatically in 2017,[3] totaling $32.56 billion. By the end of the forecast period, that share will rise to 84 percent, leaving little doubt that buyers and sellers are continuing to invest in automated ad buying. In China, programmatic ad spending will total $16.74 billion in 2017, making up more than half of China's digital display ad spending, and its increase rate rises stably as well.

FIGURE 20

By 2017, **FOUR OUT OF EVERY FIVE** US digital display dollars will transact programmatically

This will total **$32.56 BILLION** in spending.

By the end of 2017, that share will rise to **84.0%.**

In China, programmatic ad spending will total **$16.74 BILLION** in 2017, making up more than half of China's digital display ad spending.

The trend is also only growing for both mobile and native ad formats. The combination of programmatic and smart content is another emerging trend, and it's also a prime example of the merger of adtech and martech. Brands are using their first and third party data sets to target individuals with relevant content, as opposed to the earliest days of targeting when they would just serve ads to selected audience segments.

UNDERSTANDING MAJOR TECH PLAYERS

Of all of the players who are moving and shaking within the martech/adtech environment, there are five giants whose names are unavoidable: Facebook, Google, Amazon, Apple, and Microsoft. According to the Interactive Advertising Bureau, adtech revenue rose 21 percent year-on-year, but 90 percent of that growth went to Facebook and Google. These giants are also hungrily looking at martech capabilities as they start to bring in talent.

In addition to being disruptors, these five companies, at this point, also have an advantage of commanding their entire platforms. Take Facebook, for instance. It owns all of its own data and can monitor the ad experience for its 1.7 billion users. Combine this with Facebook's increased reach after acquiring both WhatsApp and Instagram, and it has an invaluable amount of information at its disposal.

Traditional adtech platforms, on the other hand, work chiefly in web territory where bots, ad blocking, and disjointed software integration run rampant.

FIGURE 21

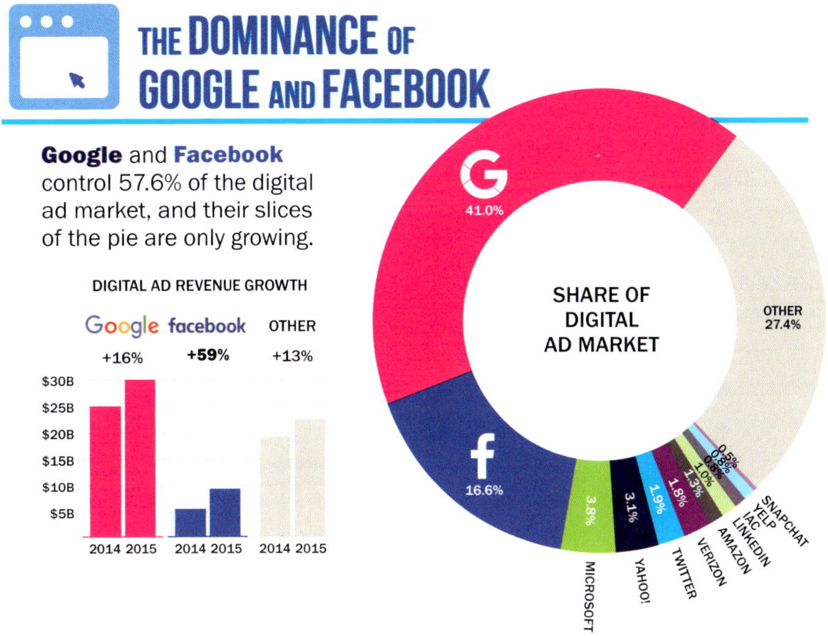

THE **DOMINANCE** OF **GOOGLE** AND **FACEBOOK**

Google and **Facebook** control 57.6% of the digital ad market, and their slices of the pie are only growing.

DIGITAL AD REVENUE GROWTH

Google facebook OTHER
+16% **+59%** +13%

SHARE OF DIGITAL AD MARKET

G 41.0%
f 16.6%
OTHER 27.4%
MICROSOFT 3.8%
YAHOO! 3.1%
TWITTER 1.9%
VERIZON 1.8%
AMAZON 1.3%
LINKEDIN 1.0%
IAC 0.6%
YELP 0.5%
SNAPCHAT

THE TOP FIVE TECH TRENDS IN MARKETING

CROSS-SCREEN STRATEGIES ARE KEY

In today's world of many screens, reaching out to customers through just one medium is no longer enough. Even if someone is watching TV, they are probably also checking social on their smartphone and shopping on their desktop at the same time. Brands are combatting consumers' multi-screen lifestyle by syncing digital buys with TVC spots, creating mobile games to be played during live television events along with responsive content to reach potential customers regardless of device.

By some measurements, mobile ad spending will account for nearly a quarter of total media spends in the coming years. As a result, brand strategy has to start with mobile; it can no longer be a secondary strategy. Many marketing campaigns are now designed for a completely mobile experience, and mobile innovation goes well beyond a temporary mobile campaign site. Brands are innovating with games, m-commerce platforms, iBeacon technology, and more as a way to stay ahead. These new technologies help brands form deeper connections with their consumers, and as a result, this has increased consumer expectations on how they interact with their favorite brands. Consumers now expect seamless integration between the digital world and what they see outside of their screens.

As more and more consumers are shifting their attention to their mobile screens, social media has become an integral part of brands' marketing strategies. Social has become more than just a tweet or creative hashtag. Marketing firms are generating interactive video and creative in-feed advertisements, using targeting and social listening tools to do never-before-seen things with the social media platforms and content. Several brands are partnering with their agencies to build social intelligence teams with an agile working method, helping them stay in the front row of the tech trends, reacting quickly on social media or adapting tech when it's still in the prototype stage.

GAMIFICATION

The process of linking products and services to an online game or competition not only showcases a brand's personality and encourages fun interactions, it allows a company to directly interact with the consumers most interested in them and gather data about their actions and preferences. It can also encourage consumers to share branded content through their own personal channels, effectively working as an amplification strategy for the brand.

Mattel, in particular, has seen great success by linking their toys and products to the digital world, allowing for personalization of their toys through gamification. Take Hot Wheels as an example. The brand released an augmented reality (AR) game called Hot Wheels Track Builder in early 2017. It allowed players to customize their race tracks, cars, and opponents. While most AR apps focus on taking images from the real world and overlaying graphical effects on a mobile screen, Track Builder focuses on creating a virtual playroom space for the player to explore physically. They can move the phone up and down and even walk around to look at the decorations and furniture in the space.

Gamification is not only for children. When done well, the combined elements of play, a points/badges system, and other incentives can be a subtle yet fun way of getting people of all ages engaged. For a good example, look no further than the Nike Fuel program, which allows runners to track their progress against others, challenge family and friends to meet fitness goals, and post their best times. In return, these enthusiasts are offered early access to products and events, free shipping, customized workouts, and more. This is a classic story of engagement in which the company is driving a deeper bond with their target audience and enhancing loyalty.

AI AND VOICE TECHNOLOGY

The industry is also on the precipice of harnessing blooming technologies, such as AI and voice-activated products. *"Another big opportunity area in technology is around voice activation. The future is voice search, voice-activated technology, and virtual digital assistants. This is a new space that we need to stay closely connected with and to build partnerships,"* says Theresa Agnew of GSK Consumer Healthcare.

CASE STUDY

gsk **THE EXCEDRIN MIGRAINE EXPERIENCE**

1 **BACKGROUND:** GSK product Excedrin Migraine is a medicine designed specifically to help migraine headache sufferers. In order to create empathy for the migraine sufferer, GSK wanted to help the spouses, friends, and co-workers of migraine sufferers to really understand what a migraine headache really feels like. An estimated 36 million Americans suffer from migraines, and the campaign's goal was to show someone who has never had a migraine before what happens when these debilitating headaches strike and how everyday tasks can become nearly impossible.

2 **PROCESS:** GSK decided to use Virtual Reality to accomplish this goal. They asked the question, "How can we use virtual reality to actually show people what a migraine sufferer goes through?" To answer, GSK launched The Migraine Experience in 2016. They used virtual reality to simulate what it's like to suffer from a migraine, with those wearing the VR headsets experiencing all the common symptoms (excluding pain), like seeing an aura or dots, as well as getting dizzy. The spots were aired on television, along with a multi-channel paid media spend across digital and social platforms. In 2017, they followed up with yet another migraine experience, which was called Excedrin Works. They used 360 video to show what a migraine sufferer might experience while having a migraine at work, with different videos for professions like pastry chef and EMT.

3 **RESULTS:** GSK made it all about the consumer who suffers from migraines, showing how it can disrupt their lives, and the reactions from their loved ones who experienced the VR migraines were captured in videos for the campaign. They successfully sought out to leverage digital technology and digital communication to create empathy for this specific segment of consumers. They saw 390k social engagements within the first three weeks of launch with an estimated 18.4k hours of brand interaction. Weber Shandwick won a Bronze Lion at Cannes for their work on The Migraine Experience Campaign. When they released the Excedrin Works videos on YouTube in 2017, they were in the top ten viral videos of the week on both YouTube and Apple.

Agnew continues, "*Artificial intelligence is another big opportunity for marketers. We like to explore different technology solutions that will help the consumer experience with our brands and with our categories.*"

Of course, solutions like Apple's Siri, Amazon's Alexa, and Google Home are already leading the charge on this. However, it's up to companies to figure out how they can best partner with these already established technologies, or break out on their own to figure out new ways in which artificial intelligence and voice activation can work for them. AI solutions don't necessarily only come in the form of smart home voice assistants. In today's new world of marketing, even an agency can be based solely on AI technology.

A start-up from Israel is working hard to reinvent the digital media planning and buying process with their AI product—Albert. By training with multiple algorithms—including predictive analytics and natural language processing to machine learning and feedback—Albert carries out almost all the tasks throughout a campaign with no human input. The most revolutionary change is that contrary to traditional media planning and buying processes (which begins with a media plan based on existing data and is relatively manual to adjust during the campaign), Albert automates the process by taking real-time input to make instant adjustments. It will decide the channel mix, creative elements, keywords, and bids to maximize campaign results. In the campaign that gave Albert its global notoriety for lingerie brand Cosabella, the brand saw a 336 percent increase in ad spend returns, and afterward declared that they are not going back to working with an ad agency. Even if this does not mean the end of media agencies, it serves as a warning for agencies to ask what value they can bring to their clients. Because for all we know, AI like Albert will only get smarter with time and training.

020

When people hear "digital" or "ad tech," they almost immediately think of being on the internet. However, many brands are creating innovative in-store experiences and using tech innovations to drive sales in brick and mortar stores rather than solely relying on e-commerce. This type of innovation ranges from in-store digital product displays, to virtual reality experiences. YH Lee of Samsung says that Samsung's technology itself is an effective way to improve the customer experience, and she says they will provide immersive online and offline retail experiences leveraging new devices, including the Samsung Gear VR, Gear 360, and digital signage.

Lee also says that Samsung stores allow potential customers to get hands-on experience with their new products, learn from their experts, and directly order products from in-store digital signage and tablets.

Another example of an O2O strategy is Shell's in-car app solution, developed with Jaguar, which lets drivers know on the navigation screen once they are within reach of a service station. Offers are pushed to the driver. Payments can be done from inside the car, as it is connected to the driver's account. Car owners can even shop products from the touchscreen in their car. *"This is the more innovative side of digitization, and then there is another side that includes digitizing existing business. Your loyalty point share, your point balance, your redemption, locations, gaming, long-term driving behavior, we have been doing these kinds of things traditionally,"* says Linda van Schaik of Shell. *"We have now digitized, modernized, and refreshed them for customers. We look at it as the development of real, new experiences as potential business models, as well as updating existing practices to today's digital standard."*

IOT

Internet of Things (IoT) has been a buzzword in the tech world for several years now, but the fact is, the world is more connected than ever before. According to an IHS survey, at the end of 2017 there were over 20 billion[4] connected devices in the world, and marketers can tap into the trend to connect with consumers in more innovative and useful ways. It's obvious that the IoT will continue to grow, but the industries that will see it flourish might not be so obvious. A recent *Forbes* article predicted that healthcare, retail, and the industrial/supply chain industries will likely see the greatest growth. It is not surprising that retail is looking to harness the power of the IoT to grow their brands and improve the customer journey in deeply personal ways. As the growth continues, the landscape will continue to fragment, giving rise to security concerns as more and more consumer data will be connected to the internet.

FIGURE 22

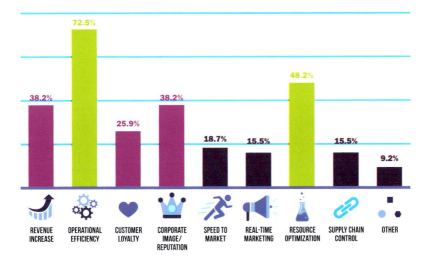

WHAT ARE THE BENEFITS OF INTEGRATING THE IoT INTO AN ORGANIZATION?

REVENUE INCREASE	38.2%
OPERATIONAL EFFICIENCY	72.5%
CUSTOMER LOYALTY	25.9%
CORPORATE IMAGE/ REPUTATION	38.2%
SPEED TO MARKET	18.7%
REAL-TIME MARKETING	15.5%
RESOURCE OPTIMIZATION	48.2%
SUPPLY CHAIN CONTROL	15.5%
OTHER	9.2%

An increasing number of marketers have already started to use the IoT for more personalized marketing efforts, such as Burger King with their "Google Home of the Whopper" campaign. The industry will have to strike a balance between personalization and intrusiveness as these connected devices will open up even more digital touchpoints on the consumer journey. Data from a recent survey of hundreds of business leaders conducted by Futurum Research[5] showed that they predict that operational efficiency will be the biggest benefit of the IoT. Just 15.5 percent of the respondents singled out real-time marketing as the biggest benefit of adopting IoT, but that number will inevitably increase when in-home connected devices start allowing advertising on these channels (which Amazon was reported[6] to have been discussing with major advertisers like P&G earlier this year).

BUILDING A TECH STACK

Brands no longer have to "cast a wide net" and hope that it reaches its target audience. The level of consumer data is at an all-time high and brands that don't take advantage of this wealth of information, either by simple targeting or a more integrated tech solution, are going to come in second place to the brands that do. Additionally, the consumers are demanding (and rewarding) this "more involved" form of marketing, along with the companies that are reaching outside the box and innovating the way they communicate with the world. It's either use tech or fall behind. The challenge is knowing the right kind of technology to integrate in the marketing mix. The landscape is vast, and sometimes confusing, and while there is a solution on the market for nearly every problem, it's up to CMOs to decide which ones are right for their brand and business.

Another big challenge that comes from all of this new technology is overwhelming consumers with content at every turn—every time they turn on their computer, look at Instagram, or interact on Facebook. This means consumers are not only overwhelmed by the content and messaging that they are receiving, but they are also going through great lengths to avoid the advertising. Meredith Verdone of Bank of America explains:

There's so much content out there, and it's content that both brands and consumers are publishing. One of the hardest statistics to take is that 95 percent of consumers are taking some actions to avoid advertising. We're in this mode of no one really being interested in our messages. The consumer attention span is what I'm really worried about. You look from generation to generation to generation, and their attention spans are getting smaller and smaller and smaller. It is so much harder to tell our message.

STAY TWO STEPS AHEAD

Brands are allocating more of their budgets and resources to digital, providing well-established brands with the opportunity to experiment with hot tech and letting fresh ideas flow to encourage constant innovation. This allows the companies to stay one step ahead of (or at least in step with) new trends. Even if a company does not invent an entirely new concept, they can improve on

FIGURE 23

A FUTURE FIT TECH STACK

PLANNING

AGENCY + SYNDICATED TOOL KIT
BUDGET ALLOCATION, PLANNING,
BUYING, BRAND AND CONSUMER
RESEARCH

MEASUREMENT
KANTAR, COMSCORE, NIELSEN

BUDGET
FLOW CHART AUTOMATION
MEDIA TOOLS, SQAD

CAMPAIGN MANAGEMENT

END TO END
SIZMEK, KENSHOO, MARIN
ADOBE, MEDIA OCEAN, CENTRO

TAG MANAGEMENT
ENSIGHTEN, GOOGLE TAG MANAGER,
TEALIUM SIGNAL, ADOBE DTM

MARKET AUTOMATION
MARKETO, SALESFORCE

AI
ALBERT, FRANK AI

BUYING

DSPs
DBM, TURN, AOL ONE
AMAZON, TUBEMOGUL, QUANTCAST,
TRADING DESK, MEDIAMATH,
ROCKETFUEL

SEARCH/SOCIAL
MARIN, SPRINKLR
KENSHOO, 4C

DATA VISUALIZATION

TABLEAU
DATORAMA
MICROSOFT

MEASUREMENT & ANALYTICS

AD VERIFICATION & BRAND SAFETY
DOUBLE VERIFY, INTEGRAL AD SCIENCE
WHITEOPS, NIELSEN, COMSCORE

VIEWABILITY
MOAT, DCM

LOCATION
FOURSQUARE, PLACED, CUEBIQ,
PLACEIQ, NINTH DECIAL

WEBSITE
GOOGLE, CRAZY EGG, ADOBE ANALYTICS,
OMNITURE, OPTIMIZELY

COMPETITIVE
PATHMATICS, KANTAR

SOCIAL
SYSOMOS, RADIAN6 (SALESFORCE),
FACEBOOK INSIGHTS

AD SERVER

SIZMEK, DCM, MEDIAMIND

CREATIVE + CONTENT
FLASHTALKING, DOUBLECLICK
INNOVID (VIDEO), ADOBE CREATIVE

PROGRAMMATIC VIDEO
VIDEOLOGY, BRIGHTROLL

DATA MANAGEMENT

DMP
TURN, BLUEKAI, KRUX
ADOBE AUDIENCE MANAGER

OTHER
LIVERAMP, TAPAD

ATTRIBUTION

MARKETSHARE, CONVERTRO,
ADOMETRY, CONVERSION LOGIC,
VISUAL IQ

what is already there. Case in point is the way Diageo is thinking about ways to move forward in the digital world.

"Specifically within the world of drinks, we are seeing changes in the way that people socialize, and this is at the heart of how we will need to adapt our marketing," says Syl Saller of Diageo. *"How will driverless cars impact the way that people spend their evenings out? How will AI help us understand individual taste preferences to allow us to bespoke distill and brew? How can wearable devices help people stay in control? These are the types of questions and a lot more that our Futures team at Diageo are working on both with our internal teams and with external start-ups across the world."*

Part of staying ahead is anticipating customer needs and making sure that both the organization's consumer-facing technology and behind-the-scenes internal technology are linked together to deliver the experience the customer wants. Axel Schwan of Burger King elaborates on this point using his experiences:

You don't want to wait too long in the drive-thru. For example, here in the US, drive-thru business is close to 70 percent, and speed of service matters. You probably know from your own experience if someone forgets an item, or if you get the wrong item—which we call order accuracy—then you're not happy. When the food is cold, you're not happy. That's why we always need to make sure that we're delivering on the basics. Then we need to think about how technology can help us to improve our accuracy, our speed of service, and our food quality. Not just the guest-facing technology, which of course we think a lot about, but also the holistic technology. One of our big goals for the future is to connect even more to the front of house and back of house so that we can deliver an even better guest experience.

ENCOURAGE PERSONAL CONNECTION

Perhaps most critical when considering which technology to invest in is to remember that new technology is not just about flash, and it's not simply a means to prove that a company is ahead of the ever-evolving digital trends. It is about fostering an ever-closer, more personal relationship with targeted consumers.

"We are evolving our approach how, when, and why we engage consumers in their daily lives, centering on the notion of driving relevancy anyway, anywhere, and anytime they choose," says Francisco Crespo of Coca-Cola. *"This requires increased segmentation capabilities that allow for greater personalization and continuity cross channels. We need the platforms that allow for faster creation and syndication of content across an ever-increasing number of touchpoints. And lastly, analytics that allow us to optimize in real time to capture maximum value."*

For Four Seasons Hotels and Resorts, deepening the relationship with their customers and strengthening brand loyalty came in the form of a new app which allows those interested in or already staying at the Four Seasons to speak directly with someone on the ground. The communication between consumer and company is not limited to one topic. For example, customers can text if they want room service at one of the hotels, if they are on their way to a hotel and want to check in early, or even if they simply want to know more about a hotel before they make a booking decision. The challenge was to create this app in a way that furthered the Four Seasons brand and did not rely on chatbot technology that creates impersonal or predetermined responses. It also required an infusion of manpower as it requires real-time reactions from real people.

Peter Nowlan of Four Seasons Hotels and Resorts explains how the app ties into the company's brand:

There's no value in technology if it doesn't enhance the Four Seasons experience for our guests—that's what drives all of our decision making in digital innovation. We're focused on investing in technology that allows a personal connection between the consumer and our people. In regard to chat, we could have launched something with a chatbot years ago. But that's not Four Seasons, and this approach didn't make sense for the level of service we needed to provide. We brought marketing, operations, and IT together to design a cross-functional chat platform that would allow consumers to connect on the channels where they were already engaging. Whether you're on the Four Seasons app, Facebook Messenger, SMS or WeChat, it all connects our guests to our people in real time. We wanted to ensure that somebody could chat with us wherever they were, whether they wanted room service in the hotel, they wanted to check in on the way to the hotel, or maybe they were just on the buying journey and wanted to know a little bit more about the hotel. We initially launched chat in ten hotels, with the majority of the portfolio now operational. We have a two-minute response time,

CASE STUDY

THE FOUR SEASONS CHAT

1 **BACKGROUND:** Following the successful launch of their app in 2015, Four Seasons was looking to evolve the product to further personalize the experience for each guest and better reflect the changing preferences of global travelers. With guests around the world embracing mobile chat applications, Four Seasons began to compile guest feedback to understand if a chat function accessible through the Four Seasons App would be a valuable tool in enhancing the guest experience. Recognizing the importance of meeting guests on the platforms where they were already engaging, the company began to explore an omni-channel approach to chat. In conceiving of a new chat service offering, Four Seasons wanted to differentiate their platform and align it with their renowned service culture by powering chat through their own people, rather than a chatbot.

2 **PROCESS:** In researching possible chat vendors, Four Seasons realized that many of the software solutions being used lacked a global approach and did not leverage some of the world's most popular platforms, including WeChat and Kakao Talk. What's more, the vendors were not suited to manage the operational variances of more than 100 hotels in more than 40 countries around the world. Four Seasons needed an option that would also meet their people-powered service requirements. The solution was to create a custom chat platform specific to Four Seasons. In early 2017, Four Seasons began piloting their custom chat platform at 30 hotels and resorts, collecting post-stay feedback from guests who used the service. During the pilot program, more than half of guests introduced to Four Seasons Chat leveraged the service on their first stay. They also engaged with Four Seasons more regularly—they averaged more than six chats during a stay, more than twice as often as the industry average of three. By the end of 2017, Chat had been rolled out to 74 hotels and resorts worldwide.

3 **RESULTS:** Four Seasons achieved their goal of developing a chat platform with a distinctive human element, one that extended their service culture by fostering connections between guests and staff that are deeply genuine and personal. Guests were engaged with the platform, and impressed with the fact that their respondents were actually on based in the hotel where they were staying. Four Seasons Chat is an omni-channel platform that can be accessed on the Four Seasons App, WeChat, Facebook Messenger, SMS, and Kakao Talk. Guests can chat to staff in more than 100 languages, with 75 percent of messages receiving responses in 90 seconds or less, well below industry averages. Chat was also successful from a guest satisfaction perspective, fostering a 25 percent increase in guest satisfaction on the mobile app, and with 51 percent chat engagement for those that were aware of the platform.

which again, is the challenge of speed. You can't be an autobot saying, 'We'll get back to you soon.' That would be distinctly un–Four Seasons.

The hospitality industry is a good example of an industry with consumers that don't necessarily want or need to constantly interface with digital technology; some still crave a more human interaction. *"We have AI, but it's hidden behind the scenes, helping to curate the information to make the personal connection easier,"* says Nowlan.

Samsung is also working to deepen personal connection, increase customer retention, and increase customer lifetime value (CLV) by strengthening their loyalty marketing strategies. *"We are building and managing 'Samsung Members' as a loyalty marketing platform in order to continue direct engagement with our customers post purchase, as well as evolve our conversations from product and feature topics to include culturally relevant topics around our customers' passion points,"* says YH Lee of Samsung. *"We are ensuring that there is a continuous journey from social media into .com, and Samsung members are led from social media campaigns into .com navigation."*

Above all, it's important to remember that there are real emotions connected to the other side of the screens, though it's more difficult to tap into them in this distracted world. *"I still think people make a lot of decisions emotionally, and having that ability to have this emotional connection in this really digital, always-on world where people are spending (if we're lucky) three seconds with your story is one of our biggest marketing challenges,"* says Meredith Verdone of Bank of America. *"That's a lot of our focus. A company like ours has the luxury of tremendous knowledge and insights about our customer base; having that ability to deeply, deeply understand them and to deliver against them."*

THE CHANGING
AGENCY MODEL

THE EVOLUTION OF CLIENT-AGENCY RELATIONSHIPS

The way that marketers and agencies work together is in a state of flux. The gold standard for client-agency relationships used to be a long-standing Agency of Record (AOR) relationship, and while there are still plenty of successful traditional relationships, the industry at large seems to be shifting away from that model. In recent years, there has been an increase in project-based work, crowdsourcing platforms, technology vendors, and even consultancies playing in the agency space that have dramatically expanded marketing organizations' options when looking for external partners. There are several different types of agency models, ranging from the "one-stop shop" all the way to "multiple best-in-class," and marketers may prefer one (or a combination) of these models based on their specific needs. One thing that has become a universal truth in the world of client-agency relationships is that there is no "one size fits all" solution when developing a way to structure a roster of external partners.

In the Mad Men era of marketing, when a company wanted to take an idea to market, the process was pretty straightforward. The creative agency would develop an idea, develop a campaign, and launch that campaign across the traditional channels: TV, print, and out-of-home (OOH). In today's digital landscape, that journey to get a message out to consumers has become increasingly complex and convoluted. Now, CMOs have to consider a wide range of digital touchpoints in addition to TV, radio, print, and OOH, and likely have a large number of agencies to coordinate in the process of developing and launching a campaign. The increased number of stakeholders also includes internal players that may not have been involved in marketing activities in the past, such as procurement, sales, data analytics, and customer service. In order to deliver a seamless consumer journey and unified brand message across the increased number of channels, CMOs have had to transform both the way they work with external partners and their organization's internal processes in order to find the right agency model that works for their marketing and business objectives.

The expanding ecosystem left many marketing organizations with a ballooning roster of agency partners. David Roman of Lenovo asserts:

Digital transformation certainly has changed the way we work with our agency partners. We have had to engage more agencies and smaller niche agencies for specific skills we need. For example, if you want to get on Instagram and your current team has no expertise on Instagram, we would engage an agency. You find small agencies that know what to do and can help you quickly develop a plan and competence in this area. As a result, we have seen an explosion in the number of agencies we are leveraging.

Some continued on with their global AORs, while others were finding that what was working on a global scale might not be translating locally, leading to not only an increased number of agency partners across disciplines, but across geographies as well. Peter Nowlan of Four Seasons Hotels and Resorts highlights the importance of their agencies being grounded in the local markets:

There is a real focus for us on in-language content as well, and that comes to the partnership discussion about how we organize to make sure that we've got agencies that really understand our brand voice in language, and can trans-create, not just translate. Conventions change by culture—and different countries are slightly different. It's all about design subtlety. And it's that wonderful balance of clearly

FIGURE 24

HOW TO GET THE MOST FROM YOUR AGENCY RELATIONSHIP IN 2017

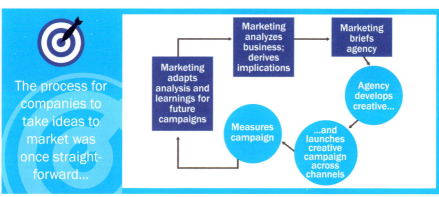

The process for companies to take ideas to market was once straight-forward...

Marketing analyzes business; derives implications → Marketing briefs agency → Agency develops creative... → ...and launches creative campaign across channels → Measures campaign → Marketing adapts analysis and learnings for future campaigns

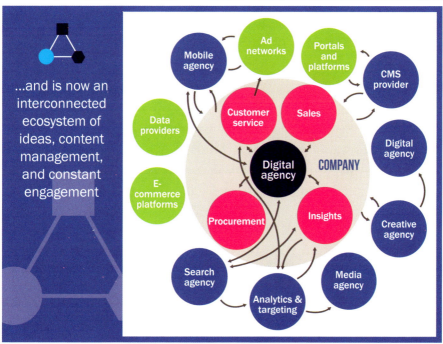

...and is now an interconnected ecosystem of ideas, content management, and constant engagement

Mobile agency · Ad networks · Portals and platforms · CMS provider · Data providers · Customer service · Sales · Digital agency · E-commerce platforms · Digital agency · COMPANY · Procurement · Insights · Creative agency · Search agency · Analytics & targeting · Media agency

One result of clients' growing and evolving needs was rising pressure on agencies to offer all-encompassing, integrated solutions, meaning that creative shops needed to boost their digital, media, and public relations (PR) offerings—as well as add market-specific talent to their teams—to meet client demands. David Timm of Pizza Hut expands on this point: "*You don't find a lot of data scientists in traditional agencies. You do find them in the e-commerce agencies. Again, somehow this will all settle down over time. I think the agency world is going to be disrupted over the next few years in order to meet the changing needs of the marketing organizations.*"

In a way, this overlap in disciplines was almost unavoidable, as the speed of change within the marketing industry in the past several decades has been incredibly difficult for agencies to keep up with. The modern concept of an integrated agency model rose out of this "digital explosion," with several factors in the marketing and communications industry driving this change.

THE ORIGINS OF INTEGRATION

For something that has been around since way back in the Mad Men days, the term integrated marketing communications (IMC) has a relatively brief history. The term was first discussed in 1989 by the American Association of Advertising Agencies, also known as the 4A's. It was also around that time that more and more agencies went public—groups such as Omnicom, WPP, and Interpublic first started forming and establishing multi-brand offerings. That was also the time period in which media independents started becoming commonplace, with Carat leading the way, followed by Mindshare, Mediacom, ZenithOptimedia, Starcom, OMD, and others throughout the 1990s.

The push toward integration has a few other root causes. The first is decreasing message impact and credibility. The growing number of commercial messages made it increasingly more difficult for a single message to have a noteworthy effect, meaning that marketers had to up their game to stand out in the crowd. The second was decreasing costs of databases. The cost of storing and retrieving names, addresses, and information from databases significantly declined, which allowed marketers to reach consumers more effectively. As clients became better educated regarding advertising policies, procedures, and tactics, they began to realize that television advertising was not the only way to reach consumers. In addition, there was a dramatic increase in the mergers and acquisitions of agencies. Many top public relations firms and advertising agencies became partners, or partnered with other communication firms. These mergers allowed for more creativity and the expansion of communications from traditional advertising to other disciplines, such as event planning and promotion. The rise of global marketing also had a role to play in creating the modern day definition of IMC. There was a rapid influx in advertising competition from foreign countries, and companies quickly realized that even if they did not conduct business outside their own country, they were now competing in global marketing.

As the development of new technology made the world smaller and smaller every year, potential customer markets exploded in size, driving companies' need for boots on the ground in local markets around the world. The increasing media and audience fragmentation from 1980 to 1990—with the exception of the decline of newspapers—meant that media outlets, such as magazines and TV stations, increased in number. Additionally, companies used new technologies and computers to target specialized audiences based on factors such as ethnic background or place of residence. Lastly, the dramatic increase in the number of overall products on the market meant that CMOs needed a unique marketing and branding approach to attract customer attention and increase sales. As a result of these changes, the way that clients and agencies worked together inevitably changed as well.

In R3's recent study of integration, titled Integration 40, the Six Degrees of Integration were identified as the six most common agency models to emerge from this rapidly changing marketplace.

In reality, integration in today's marketing landscape usually involves multidisciplined teams working together on a single idea and approach. There is no silver lining to having multiple agencies aligned and working together; it takes a lot of patience, diplomacy, and the right motivation. There are several key factors that contribute to a successful integration strategy, including defining a clear chain of command, which is often best managed directly by the CMO. Such is

FIGURE 25

R3'S SIX DEGREES OF INTEGRATION

Multiple- Best in Class Agencies

Client hires multiple agency specialists across different disciplines (creative, media, digital, PR, multicultural, etc.). **Examples:** Most marketers use this approach.

Lead Agency

Client hires "lead agency" to provide overall brand direction, helps client manage and coordinate other agency resources. **Examples:** P&G (BAL model), Huawei, some others.

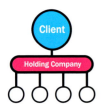

Holding Company- Sibling Agency Solution

Client serviced through agency holding company; team of discipline specialists, usually with one agency in lead. **Examples:** Visa, Reckitt Benckiser, Clorox, HSBC, HP, IBM

Holding Company- Custom Agency

Holding company creates custom agency for the client. **Examples:** Dell (short-lived), Apple, Ford, Nestle (some markets)

Free Agent

Client draws from multiple and varying agency resources as needed (few, if any, formal AOR or retainer assignments). **Examples:** Intel, Sony

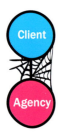

One Stop Shop- (Single Agency)

One agency hired to do everything; unlike the "custom agency," this is an established agency that can handle multiple marketing/advertising functions. **Examples:** Common for smaller clients or B2B marketers Common in Japan, Korea, Brazil the case with Raja Rajamannar of Mastercard, who says, *"What I have is a top to top connection between me and the agency chief."*

Maryam Banikarim of Hyatt Hotels echoes that sentiment, saying, *"All agencies are looking for a bigger piece of the pie, so it's important to set ground rules about how the agencies should work together. Each agency comes with different disciplines and that is advantageous, but you still need to designate a lead so they don't trip over each other."*

Another important driver of integration is training. Leading companies are investing as much as ten percent of their marketing team time into training—learning about social media, the power of search, best practices in media contact strategies—and a number of other areas. Last, and perhaps most important, is promoting accountability through robust measurable action.

EMERGING TRENDS IN CLIENT-AGENCY RELATIONSHIPS

This rapid push toward integration and the fragmentation of the marketing and media landscape has significantly altered the client-agency relationship working model. The models are constantly changing and evolving, but there are several trends that seem to be emerging from the fray.

One of the most significant trends emerging from marketers on their agency relationships is the race to eliminate inefficiencies. In the past year, a growing number of marketers have sought to create an agency model that improves process efficiencies while eliminating unnecessary costs. As evidenced by recent marketing trade press interviews with the likes of Unilever CMO Keith Weed, big advertisers are looking to eliminate waste, and Unilever isn't the only global CPG to take on this challenge. In early 2017, Procter & Gamble also announced their intention to cut $2 billion in agency and media costs. Whether marketers are looking to cut the overall number of agencies they work with or—in the case of another large global CPG company—are seeking to evaluate their relationship with their one agency to identify possible improvements, the message to agencies is clear: shape up or ship out. Marketers are taking several different approaches to address the inefficiencies affecting their bottom lines, from completely reorganizing their agency compensation structure to building in-house agencies in place of external partners. Some of the push to build up in-house capabilities is being driven by the rise of new technology. David Roman of Lenovo speaks to this point:

However, we are also seeing a trend in the industry around doing things in house and developing in house agencies. This is something we are studying and [we] are focused on trying to do more things in-house. There are some things that inevitably will just be easier to do in-house, but the role of the agencies is still absolutely there. Our key creative agency is Ogilvy, which is still really driving all of our creative work that ends up in digital or traditional media. We've now got a tighter portfolio of digital and social agencies, and so I think the situation is continuing to evolve.

Another important trend revolves around changing agency compensation models. The move toward a value-based compensation model is something expected to take off in the next few years. This model can be applied to nearly any type of client-agency relationship because the method for arriving at value is independent of agency input costs; it is arrived at based on business value drivers as determined by the marketer. In this type of fee structure, the agency's compensation is usually tied to accomplishing a specific marketing or business goal, which means that both party's success or failure is inextricably linked. Cola-Cola switched over to this compensation model in 2009, and now with Unilever's acknowledgment that it has started using this model as well, we expect to see many marketers following suit.

One interesting trend is increase in the free agent model. In the Mad Men era, it was very common for a marketer to award their entire business to one agency or holding group, allowing them to handle all aspects of the business globally. Today, rather than taking a one size fits all model and applying it to all the business units across all geographical markets, CMOs are picking and choosing the successful elements of different types of working models and drawing from a variety of resources to meet their diversifying needs. What works in the US might not be successful in China, and a global creative AOR may simply not have the talent to produce a localized VR or AR campaign. Weed of Unilever has revealed in recent interviews that they are in the process of cutting Unilever's 3,000 agency roster in half, focusing in on specialized and locally relevant agencies while cutting out shops that weren't offering differentiation.

In a similar vein, marketers are also turning to crowdsourced, independent networks rather than holding companies or traditional agencies to fulfill some of their marketing needs. There is so much demand for content among consumers today, and any agency that tries to offer it all will find themselves burning the candle at both ends. Brands are increasingly turning to the likes of CreativeDrive, a group of content specialists who help clients align their content creation cycle with the transformation of the media landscape and digital marketing as a whole to fulfill their special content needs. Speakeasy, another crowdsourcing platform, connects brands to freelance creative teams via their online brief creation tool, allowing them to work with top talent "without barriers." Similar networks are springing up for project-based technology work, such as Alphachannel, that helps clients source proposals from specialists in chatbots, AR, VR, user experience/user interface (UX/UI) design, Amazon Echo, and several other fields. These types of small players are successfully bridging a gap that has been growing over the past few years, as some large agencies have been slow to onboard talent who are up to date in latest digital and technology trends. While crowdsourcing creativity is not a new concept, it is only going to become more popular going forward as the idea of "may the best idea win" has really taken hold in the industry. Some marketers realize that agencies are facing a difficult task. *"We expect agencies to be subject matter experts, but on the other hand have the breadth to be able to understand the big picture,"* says Andres Kiger of Converse. *"It almost sounds like I'm contradicting myself by looking for narrow skills but broad capacity. We are all looking for that partner that has both the creative ability to crack the code but also the operational knowledge to land the plane."*

BEST PRACTICES FROM GLOBAL MARKETERS

Even amongst all the change and uncertainty in the client-agency relationship space, there are many global players who are getting it right. The CMOs that participated in this book are putting best practices into place within their own organizations in both their day-to-day interactions with their agency partners, as well as their long-term strategies.

CASE STUDY

Lenovo. GOODWEIRD

1 **BACKGROUND:** Lenovo's multi-year campaign dubbed "Goodweird" initially focused on a tablet computer with a built-in high-definition video projector. However, its end goal was to push the idea that innovations that become familiar and a part of everyday life still initially came across as strange. The campaign came to life in 2015 and is still going strong today, using a three-pronged approach of leveraging influencers, crowdsourcing ideas, and co-creating content. The success of Goodweird is largely centered around the external partners used to create the campaign, which involves multiple agencies and other players.

2 **PROCESS:** Lenovo worked with three different agencies to deploy their Goodweird campaign. London-based creative house DLKW Lowe came up with the slogan, while We Are Social handled all of the social media aspects and Blast Radius took on the digital marketing. At the time of the launch, Lenovo's VP of Global Brand Strategy acknowledged the need to embrace a different agency model, stating that "once the idea came out it, it was a lot easier to rally them around a single idea and they eventually worked very closely together to roll this out." As the campaign evolved over the next several years, the tech giant involved other players, like Vice Media, to co-create content and keep the campaign relevant.

3 **RESULTS:** Just after the campaign's launch in 2015, #goodweird was the third highest hashtag for brand discussion with more than 10,000 retweets. Lenovo's integrated campaign extended beyond their typical brand audience, and helped to convert fans in the wider millennial segment. In their most recent series of videos produced by Vice Media, the videos garnered 45 million views, 27k engagements, and a 55 percent completion rate within the first six weeks, and 550k people clicked on to Lenovo.com.

THE SECRETS OF SUCCESSFUL GLOBAL MARRIAGE

LOOK TO NEW MODELS

Successful global marketers like P&G, Coca-Cola, and Unilever share one thing in common: they continue to evolve. They continue to keep their client-agency marriages fresh. Whether it's outcome-based compensation, IMC innovation, or the brand agency leader model, the best brands trust their lead agency to manage others and drive business, with some resulting in very long relationships. For example, P&G and Grey, Publicis, Saatchi, and Leo Burnett have more than 50 years together. *"The way we work with our agencies has completely changed,"* says Theresa Agnew of GSK Consumer Healthcare. She continues:

With the digital transformation that we've done in the last four years in the US, I would say we operate extremely differently than we did previously. We have changed our marketing mix, the comprehensive approach that we now take, and the way we work with our agencies. We have dedicated integrated agency teams that work directly with the brand teams and internal discipline experts across social, content/digital agency, shopper, creative, public relations, and media. We take a holistic approach to how we develop our 360 activations because the consumer journey has changed. It's not linear anymore. It's essential that we keep all our agencies team-oriented and acting as one well-informed, integrated team. When we conduct a 360 activation, we're doing something in social that's connected to what we're doing in PR, that's connected to what we're doing in shopper, and with our overall creative strategy.

While this approach is not new in the industry, it is new to GSK over the past few years and Agnew says it has completely transformed how GSK works with its agency partners.

There is no silver bullet for finding the right agency model. It comes along with trying new things to see what works and what doesn't. The answer will be different for every CMO, and even successful agency models will still have challenges for both parties. *"We have a unique agency model that is very good for us, but it also poses challenges,"* says Mukul Deoras of Colgate-Palmolive. *"It is good because there are no conflicting multiple agency P&L's distracting us, there is single-point brand knowledge, ownership and accountability. We don't need to align*

> *"We really challenge our partners in the agency to not think TV, but to think digital first. To think about narrative and storytelling. To think about purpose and things that matter to consumers in terms of relevance. It's been a real shift in moving away from traditional methods of communication to having a digital first mindset. Digital has become so synonymous with how we operate that it's like the air that we breathe."*
>
> **JULIANA CHUGG**
> *Mattel*

20 different teams. We have one set of people and everything is aligned with that one set, and that works for us. But because of our model, we have to constantly focus on accessing the best talent from the holding company in a far more flexible manner."

FACE TIME MATTERS

Whether it's through the use of technology or through physical presence, the best global relationships are not conducted solely through email and PowerPoint. Getting people together can make all the difference in the world. Some marketers fix these times quarterly, others on a key project basis. Raja Rajamannar of Mastercard revealed that he includes the brand's agency partners in all of their strategy meetings. Each CMO needs to find the right cadence for them, and make it work. In the best global relationships, both sides spend time to become immersed in the other. For an agency, this could be joining the sales team for a supermarket run, or it could mean working in the store, or even just becoming an active consumer of the client's products. For a client, this also needs to happen: attending the agency's office to listen to work, understanding their new developments, and becoming an advocate for them. The result will be a stronger foundation. For Axel Schwan of Burger King, the agency relationship is much more than a purely transactional one. *"The moment you bring on an agency partner from the outside, you want to make sure you treat them like they are on the inside, because they are,"* he says. Linda Boff of GE echoes that sentiment, particularly because GE has such a small internal marketing team that external partners are really valued assets. *"We are a really small, global corporate marketing group of fewer than 20 people. That's really, really small. The reason I make that point is because we treasure our agency partnerships because they're our extended teams, literally,"* says Boff.

TAKE DIGITAL SERIOUSLY

Digital relationships can be a minefield of challenges. Too many marketers hire their digital agencies by the yard, not by the year. So digital agencies, for the most part, usually don't see the need to invest in strategic planning or analytics, since neither side knows how long the relationship will last. Everything is so new, so everything tends to be more short term. Juliana Chugg of Mattel has played an active role in pushing their current agency partners to embrace digital. She says:

We really challenge our partners in the agency to not think TV, but to think digital first. To think about narrative and storytelling. To think about purpose and things that matter to consumers in terms of relevance. It's been a real shift in moving away from traditional methods of communication to having a digital first mindset. Digital has become so synonymous with how we operate that it's like the air that we breathe.

BENCHMARK AND EVALUATE

Marketers and agencies should be using external measures, whether it's tracking research, media audits, 360-degree performance evaluations, or other measures to benchmark where they are in an ever-changing marketplace. It doesn't have to just be through a pitch. In R3's consulting experience, we have seen one client that audits their agency every year—and seven years later, there's still been no pitch. While the relationship is not totally perfect, there's a lot of continuity and consistency. Johnson & Johnson is one marketing organization that does evaluations better than just about anyone else, actively asking agencies for feedback on how they can become a better client. In the words of Mastercard CMO, Raja Rajamannar, *"Problems happen all the time…but we solve them with a lot of openness, transparency and collaboration."* This mindset is key to a successful long-term client-agency relationship. There will always be problems that need solving and pain points along the way, but ensuring that each stakeholder is getting the most that they can from the relationship, there needs to be a framework put in place to measure success.

PAIN POINTS IN GLOBAL AGENCY MANAGEMENT

Managing a global agency relationship does not come without its challenges. When integrating a large number of stakeholders across business units and geographies, sometimes things can get complicated. The rise of new players in the agency space has left many in the agency world worried about new competitors. Meredith Verdone of Bank of America points out:

I think that whole industry is being disrupted and agencies are trying to find their way. You've got publishers now acting as agencies and they have full creative capabilities. You've got brands that are also content creators. Then you've got all these new entrants—whether it's the Accentures, the Deloittes, or the McKinseys all getting in who are either digitally focused, data focused, or creative focused. Now that everything is digital, what happens with your traditional agency?

This trend has been on the rise in the past several years, with more and more diverse players coming into the marketing mergers and acquisitions space, acquiring agencies to boost their creative or digital expertise. The entrance of these new players has agencies feeling the pressure to beef up internal capabilities and making profit margins razor-thin to face the coming wave of new competition.

Making sure all partners in an integrated model are aligned is one of the key drivers to success. *"How you integrate your agencies is key—Hyatt is a multi-brand player, and we want our agencies to understand our business and how our brands serve various customer segments. You are only as good as your agency partners. So knowing how to manage them and how to be a good client is key,"* says Maryam Banikarim of Hyatt Hotels. Driving alignment from the top down is important, making the CMO a key player in making sure that agency teams are working together across disciplines, and with internal brand teams as well. Mukul Deoras of Colgate-Palmolive also highlights the difficulty of aligning partners, especially in this fragmented landscape:

In the past, it was reasonably black and white—much simpler. You had one flow chart where you could see what you're trying to achieve throughout the year. Now, you are throwing a lot of things in the pot, and it has implications on what is delivered to the consumers. It also has implications on what creative content gets produced because content production is also becoming extremely fragmented. There needs to be brand consistency that you can see across content. It is this complexity in digital transformation where you need very strong leadership on the agency level to form a holistic picture of what goes to the consumers, how it gets created, and how it can remain consistent. It requires a very different kind of leadership to make that happen. And I believe our agency model actually helps us tremendously.

Burnout is also a concern for agency talent. It is important to keep teams fresh, energized, and focused on delivering the best creative and the newest tools and solutions. *"With long-term brand-agency relationships, the burnout rate can be significant, and it's crucial to challenge agency partners to move talent around and ensure that those on the account are still feeling good about the work and not worn out,"* says Jennifer Breithaupt of Citi.

THE FUTURE OF CLIENT-AGENCY RELATIONSHIPS

It's safe to say that the rapid speed of digital transformation, coupled with the rise of crowdsourcing networks and questions about transparency, will have an effect on client-agency relationships going forward. One thing that is certain is agencies are still an integral part of an organization's marketing structure, and even with all the recent upheaval to agency models, that likely won't change any time soon. *"Moving forward, Samsung will work closely with agencies to fully utilize new innovations to further strengthen our marketing campaigns and activations,"* says YH Lee of Samsung. Marketers will likely (and should) examine their agency contracts more closely to make media practices more transparent. There might also be an increase in bringing some capabilities in-house when it makes sense for the marketing function to do so.

How much a marketing department can take in-house varies drastically case by case. Some very "traditional" marketers, such as luxury fashion houses, tend to take on more marketing in-house to maintain complete creative control over both the brand message and consumer relationships. For the most part, these companies have their own in-house creative directors who want efficiency and consistency. The massive shift to both digital marketing and e-commerce has been a huge challenge to many luxury brands in recent years, because they are trying to move into the online space while still maintaining the exclusivity of luxury, all while attempting to keep the marketing function close to home.

On the other end of the spectrum, more experimental brands tend to take more risks in everything, not just their marketing. The frustration of not being able to find the right expertise externally can spur the decision to build in-house expertise, with cost rarely being the driver of this decision. They often believe that they provide a fertile canvas to attract and retain best talent. Meredith Verdone of Bank of America feels that agencies have an important role to play in their marketing mix. *"I'm a strong believer that external agencies have an important role. It's important to have an external perspective,"* says Verdone. *"We have about a 200-person shop down in Wilmington that does a lot of our in-house, and I would say we have brought some things in over the years. But that has not been my focus to dramatically insource things."* Raja Rajamannar of Mastercard echoes that sentiment, saying, *"I cannot afford to have all of the talent inside the company, and the agency is a fantastic talent resource, so let me leverage them in a very positive way."*

Many marketers are hoping to move into the digital future together with their agencies, creating a culture where there is mutual digital transformation. *"We're at the beginning of the journey,"* says David Timm of Pizza Hut. *"I think as much as we're struggling and working out how to do this, I feel that, if anything, our agency partners are behind us in leading the transformation. We're working with them now and creating an expectation that we want them to be pulling us into the future, not holding us back."* While some CMOs have left their long-standing agency partners in search of smaller, more nimble digital players, many of the world's largest marketing organizations have doubled-down on their existing relationships, finding that the agency's deep knowledge of their business will be a huge advantage going forward. For example, Mars and BBDO (a worldwide advertising agency network based in New York City) have been working together for 80 years. Mars CMO Andrew Clarke says:

I have to say I'm pleased with the progress. I think when I came into the CMO role, a number of people, including senior people in Mars, were expecting me to make some different choices with our agency partners. Actually, I've gone the other way. I've doubled down with the partnerships and actually have been demanding of what I expect from them. They evolved their model and their support for us, but I believe that long term partnership and that knowledge of our business is a competitive advantage.

LOOK TO ASIA

Asia is an incredibly large region that can create both opportunities and challenges for global companies trying to stay consistent across regions, and for regional marketers looking to expand. The region itself is widely diverse, leading to unique challenges that require extra vigilance from global CMOs and their teams. It is also an extremely digitally advanced market, rife with local pioneers and with room for innovation and new ways to reach out to consumers.

KEEPING UP WITH ASIA'S CONSUMERS

Statistics on the Asia-Pacific market can be overwhelming. They reflect a massive and upwardly mobile population, with rising disposable personal income estimated to have grown at an average annual rate of 11.5 percent in China, 6.6 percent in Vietnam, and 5.7 percent in Malaysia[1] alone. In addition to this growing income (along with the already powerful incomes of more mature markets like Japan, South Korea, and Singapore), there are many more millions expected to land firmly in the middle class in the coming years, while millions of people will be coming out of poverty in the near future.

FIGURE 26

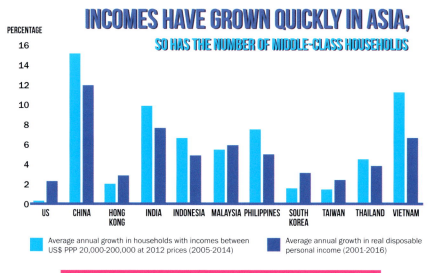

INCOMES HAVE GROWN QUICKLY IN ASIA;
SO HAS THE NUMBER OF MIDDLE-CLASS HOUSEHOLDS

PERCENTAGE

Legend:
- Average annual growth in households with incomes between US$ PPP 20,000-200,000 at 2012 prices (2005-2014)
- Average annual growth in real disposable personal income (2001-2016)

Note: Figures for India, Indonesia, the Philippines, and Thailand; 2015 figure for Vietnam; and 2016 figures for all countries are estimates by Oxford Economics

This range of market maturity leads to the need for a variety of localization techniques which can differ from country to country, and even from city to city. The way products are positioned and marketed across the region must be in line with these divides.

The extreme differences in development can lead to challenges outside of marketing, including supply chain and delivery logistics. Markets like South Korea, Singapore, and Japan tend to have well-planned cities and exceptional infrastructure, allowing for economies of scale in a modern trade environment. Other markets like Thailand, Vietnam, and Malaysia are split, offering both modern retail channels (often in cities) and more fragmented options in rural areas.

On the industry side, regional companies are steadily rising to meet demand both at home and around the world. In the "BrandZ Top 100 Most Valuable Global Brands,"[2] 24 brands from the APAC region made it into the top list, including Tencent at number eight and Alibaba and China Mobile at 14 and 17, respectively.

FIGURE 27

BRANDZ TOP 100 MOST VALUABLE
GLOBAL BRANDS 2017 IN ASIA

In 2017, 24 brands from the APAC region made it into the BrandZ™ Top 100 Most Valuable Global Brands, of which 13 were Chinese, and Tencent was the only one to crack the top 10 list.

8	*Tencent* 腾讯		61	中国平安 PING AN
14	Alibaba Group 阿里巴巴集团		64	MOUTAI
17	中国移动 China Mobile		72	中国农业银行 AGRICULTURAL BANK OF CHINA
28	ICBC 圏		78	中国人寿 CHINA LIFE
39	Baidu 百度		85	Sinopec
49	HUAWEI		94	中国银行 BANK OF CHINA
54	中国建设银行 China Construction Bank			

THE REST OF APAC CONTRIBUTED 11 MORE:

30	TOYOTA		88	T
37	SAMSUNG		91	HONDA
50	NTT		95	SoftBank
60	Commonwealth Bank		97	AIA THE REAL LIFE COMPANY
63	HDFC BANK		100	NISSAN
75	ANZ			

Another interesting disconnect throughout Asia is that, even though it's one of the most digitally forward places in the world, innovating and adopting new technologies at a higher rate than many other mature markets, there are also pockets in which internet penetration is quite low. While South Korea and Japan have an internet penetration of 92 and 93 percent respectively, China (with its population of 1.4 billion) has a mere 52 percent penetration, and Indonesia 50 percent.[3] This gives rise to great growth potential but also a disconnect in the way people are interacting with the digital world.

FIGURE 28

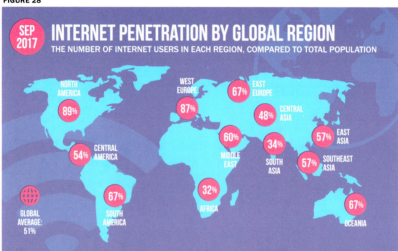

FIGURE 29

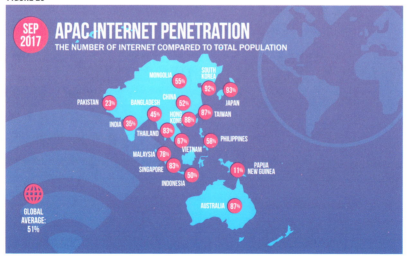

The mismatched rate of development poses a unique set of challenges to brands. Particularly brands in the quick service restaurants (QSR) category where disposable income and cultural food preferences deeply influence sales. *"We're a complex business. We're in 105 markets around the world, and they have matured at different rates leading to technology differences and gaps around the world,"* says David Timm of Pizza Hut. *"The extent to which the business is online versus offline differs around the world. Our capabilities differ around the world. Yes, pacing and sequencing is pretty tough. I think, like all businesses, you've got to be embracing the future and still delivering what you're doing today to drive short-term sales."*

FIGURE 30

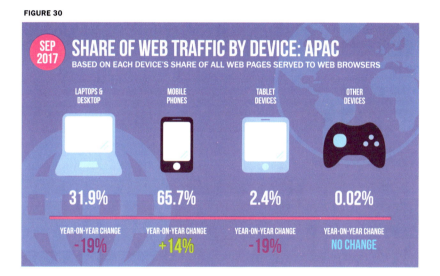

A LOVE FOR NEW TECHNOLOGIES

On the flip side of the development coin, Asia is also more enthusiastic about and open to adopting new technologies and digital platforms into their everyday lives. Many of these countries have only really been in the throes of economic development for the past 30 years, allowing them to leap-frog over outdated legacy technologies that most Western nations are currently struggling to update. An example would be China's enthusiasm to adopt mobile payment platforms. They went from a largely cash society to mobile payments seemingly overnight, skipping the transition from cash to card that other countries went through.

Another example of the willingness of Asia's consumers to adopt new technology is that Indian and Chinese consumers are more keen about connected devices in the home than other international markets. In a Mindshare survey of 11,000 respondents across 19 countries, the proportion of "very interested" from these two markets far exceeded the global average.[4]

This same enthusiasm can be found for VR and AR technology, which can offer interactive shopping, education, or brand engagement experiences from industries as wide-ranging as retail, education, and travel. Research from Worldpay[5] in 2017 found that 95 percent of survey respondents in China said they've used VR or AR technology in the past three months, indicating growing interest. Two-thirds of Japanese consumers surveyed said they would like to see more physical stores use VR and AR, while 84 percent of Chinese respondents said they believed VR and AR would be the future to shopping. This reflects a broad and eager audience who are avid about digital enhancement in their everyday consumer experience.

CONTENT MARKETING IS THRIVING, BUT INCONSISTENT

Companies in Asia-Pacific are increasing their marketing budgets and are reporting better ROI, and it seems content marketing is a key contributing factor. An Asia Pacific Content Marketing Trend's Report[6] by Hubspot found that 49 percent of Asia Pacific (APAC) businesses increased their marketing budgets in 2016, with the majority believing that content marketing is the greatest factor in their marketing success.

That same survey of 720 marketers across the APAC region discovered 47 percent of APAC companies determined that blogs and articles are the most effective type of content marketing. This was followed by e-newsletters at 35 percent, which seemed to create a more personal connection with the consumer, leading to excellent ROI.

Despite this, companies in Asia are still trying to figure out how to better measure effectiveness. While they are producing more content, they are also still working out how to produce better *quality* content. That same survey by Hubspot found that 57 percent of marketers reported that producing quality content was an obstacle to success, and 70 percent felt that their content marketing efforts were limited, basic, or inconsistent. This shows a disconnect for marketers in Asia between analyzing what is effective and acting on it. This means there are opportunities to refine and master content marketing in each of the different markets. Use global markers, but keep an eye on local habits and movements.

VIDEO IS KING

In addition to more traditional content like blogs and articles, Asia has an affinity for video content. eMarketer predicted that digital video viewership in Asia-Pacific would increase by 10.3 percent year over year (YoY) in 2017,[7] with 569 million digital video viewers in China alone. However, despite this impressive number, the total population penetration for digital video viewership across the APAC region is actually lower than other regions worldwide due to low broadband accessibility and high population counts, despite the fact that local players like iQiyi are beginning to offer more and more on-demand video options. Like with traditional content, this leaves a lot of room for growth in the region and shows that video engagement is likely to rise, and marketers' strategies are already reflecting this change. Programmatic digital video ad spending in China alone rose to $2.01 billion in 2017, and video's share of total programmatic digital display ad spending is expected to increase to 12 percent in 2018, about three times the 4.2 percent share it had in 2014.

CHINA VERSUS THE REST OF THE REGION

Of all the countries in Asia, China is one of the most difficult to conquer. Achieving success there is an incredible feat, but it is challenging due to the isolated digital ecosystem and the vast cultural differences between China and the Western world. The past 30 years has seen the country develop at such a terrific pace that today's Chinese consumers have essentially skipped over the computer era and rely almost solely on their cell phones for internet access. China is unique in that it doesn't have many legacy systems or processes to overcome and can "play leapfrog" to innovate in the digital space faster than in the US. Therefore, the digital ecosystem is both richer and more dynamic than that of other countries. In addition, due to a robust firewall and government-funded internet platforms, the digital ecosystem is markedly different than that of other countries, with major Western players falling victim either to censorship or protectionism.

FIGURE 31

DIGITAL VIDEO VIEWERS AND PENETRATION IN ASIA-PACIFIC, 2016-2020
BILLIONS, % CHANGE AND % OF INTERNET USERS

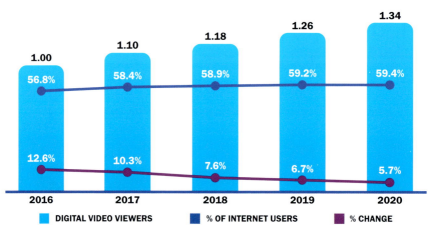

NOTE: INTERNET USERS OF ANY AGE WHO WATCH STREAMING OR DOWNLOADED VIDEO CONTENT VIA ANY DEVICE AT LEAST ONCE PER MONTH

The massive, mobile-native population has experienced a continual growth of purchasing power, and global marketers without a China strategy are missing out on the world's largest consumer market.

"When it comes to China, you have to spend time understanding today's Chinese customer. You have to be familiar with the different tools they depend on—for example, WeChat to communicate, browse, and shop—which may not be the ones you use personally," says Maryam Banikarim of Hyatt Hotels. *"We know that the Chinese customer is traveling more than ever, both in-country and internationally. We also know that the middle class in China has been growing. So, in order to better care for them, we need to know what matters to them and proactively meet and exceed their expectations at every turn."*

FIGURE 32

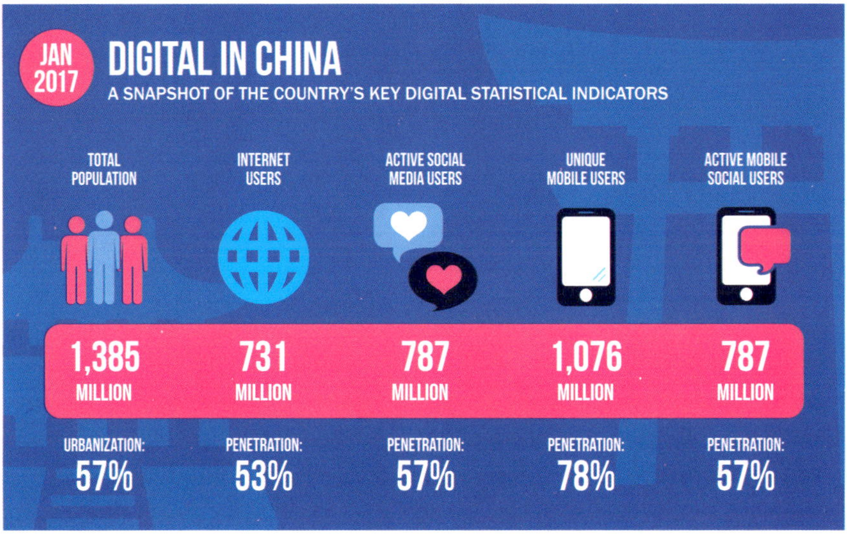

JAN 2017

DIGITAL IN CHINA

A SNAPSHOT OF THE COUNTRY'S KEY DIGITAL STATISTICAL INDICATORS

TOTAL POPULATION	INTERNET USERS	ACTIVE SOCIAL MEDIA USERS	UNIQUE MOBILE USERS	ACTIVE MOBILE SOCIAL USERS
1,385 MILLION	731 MILLION	787 MILLION	1,076 MILLION	787 MILLION
URBANIZATION: 57%	PENETRATION: 53%	PENETRATION: 57%	PENETRATION: 78%	PENETRATION: 57%

THE DOMINATION OF BAT(X)

Of the proliferation of Chinese-born technology companies that are changing the global landscape, perhaps none are as powerful as the all-important BAT group: Baidu, Alibaba, and Tencent. Many now include connected device and smartphone manufacturer Xiaomi in that list, calling the group BATX. The four giants have a combined market capitalization of around $900 billion[8] and have incubated more than 1,000 new ventures in the past ten years. They are not only immensely financially successful, but they also have a deep understanding of the market they are serving. For example, Xiaomi overtook Apple in the Chinese market just four years after its establishment, and even Baidu is making great strides into AI, in some ways that surpass even Google and Facebook.

BAT is also disrupting client-agency relationships in China, where marketers have been increasingly moving their business from media agencies and taking their dollars directly to the platforms Baidu, Tencent, and Alibaba. From a cost perspective, the thought process revolves around the concept of cutting out the middleman. If the platforms are willing to negotiate good rates directly with the marketers, why would they pay an agency to do the same? The other major driver of this trend is transparency. Agency trading desks in China are largely seen as a complete black box, and fears about how agencies are spending their money are driving marketers to move media buying in-house. China is truly a supply-side media market, so the buying power of agencies is relatively weak. It is worth noting that programmatic is just a small portion of what a media shop does for clients. R3's 2016 Agency Scope Study found that, while specialist media shops continue to lead media planning and buying, there is an increasing in-house involvement: 59 percent of the 405 marketers surveyed are closely involved with their media planning, and 46 percent are leading media buying.

Tencent's bread and butter, WeChat, has more than 1 billion users worldwide and has become an integral part of Chinese consumers' everyday lives. It has evolved far beyond its original function as a chat platform, and it now functions as social media, chatting, and e-commerce platforms all rolled into one interface. Chinese consumers use WeChat countless times throughout the day whether they are shopping, paying for dinner, calling a taxi, splitting a bill, messaging a friend, booking a train ticket, paying their electricity bills, or making a phone call.

WeChat in particular has opened the door for nimble, digitally savvy organizations whose focus has shifted away from the "traditional" online marketing models of banner ads and paid social. WeChat can be used in so many diverse ways, like helping brands reach consumers across several different touchpoints in their consumer journeys. It can also help to facilitate the sales process, taking out the traditional step of cold-calling, and making the follow-up process more natural since the consumers have already been engaged at one digital touchpoint inside the app.

LEVERAGING KOLS

When it comes to the social environment of China, perhaps one of the first things to understand is the impressive amount of power held by key opinion leaders (KOLs). While KOLs are relatively ubiquitous across the global advertising universe, the trend of leveraging celebrities or other key internet personalities to drive traffic and sales is particularly popular—and effective—in China. According to research from a recent R3 report, there are several types of KOL agencies that have risen in China to meet this demand. There are KOL search platforms that help brands identify the right influencers and the right platforms, there are typical social media agencies that developed relationships with KOLs, and then there's a third kind called the KOL incubator (or an agency that invests in and promotes KOLs).

A great example of this type of agency is EJAM. They are truly focused on social with a four-pronged approach to the platform: social marketing integration, media placement strategy, social media operation, and performance-based advertising. A major component of EJAM's KOL strategy is what they refer to as "content incubation." This means that the agency invests in the development of WeChat official accounts, as distributing brand content on these channels have a far greater reach than simply posting on a brand channel. This differs from the traditional definition of KOL in the sense that a KOL is usually a celebrity or an individual person. In EJAM's case, the focus is put heavily on the development of popular WeChat channels. EJAM's library of official accounts numbers more than 10,000, covering over 190 million WeChat users. Focusing on creating a new media business platform based on these WeChat official accounts, EJAM aims to provide a one-stop shop that covers everything from gathering new media information, to resource matching and creative advertising, to marketing execution and performance tracking with data analysis.

E-COMMERCE, M-COMMERCE, AND S-COMMERCE

Chinese consumers have taken e-commerce to new heights, integrating online purchasing into nearly every aspect of their digital journeys. Two specific types of e-commerce, mobile commerce (m-commerce) and social commerce (s-commerce), have steadily been on the rise in China. Making purchases via mobile apps is incredibly popular. For example, on Single's Day (the Chinese equivalent of Black Friday) in 2016, 82 percent[9] of Chinese consumers shop on their mobile phones. The US is lagging far behind in comparison, with only 36 percent of Americans making purchases on their mobile phones on Black Friday of 2017. Because of the legacy of personal computer-based e-commerce—which China totally skipped over—consumers in the United States are far behind their Chinese contemporaries. According to Statista,[10] there will be 2.1 billion smartphone users worldwide by 2021, meaning that more and more people will inevitably shop on their phones. In China, m-commerce is already very sophisticated, including functions like mobile money transfers, coupons, content purchasing and delivery, loyalty cards, ticketing, vouchers, and more.

In China, e-commerce is already fully integrated with social media platforms, particularly WeChat. Companies can sell directly to their consumers using the platform's built-in payment system, and the app has become a central tool that can handle both customer engagement and commerce. The entire purchasing funnel can be realized on WeChat, as brands can socialize with consumers, have one-on-one interactions, answer customer services questions, make sales, and follow up post-sale all in one place.

Another big e-commerce trend in China in the last several years has been the rise of O2O (online to offline, or vice versa), in which retailers are using digital to drive in-store purchases. In today's marketing landscape, online and offline need to be integrated together and not placed into silos in order to ensure a seamless purchasing experience. O2O strategies can have several benefits. Driving consumers into physical stores can help them feel more connected to the brand, and today's consumer craves a truly seamless shopping experience, so integrating digital aspects into brick and mortar stores has also been successful. It can also be a logistical strategy. For example, during the last Single's Day in China, Alibaba virtually merged physical stores' stocks with online shops' stocks so consumers were delivered the nearest stock and there was less chaos in the delivery process. O2O can thus help e-commerce retailers save time and money with better logistics by leveraging physical stores as part of their supply chain, thus cutting the costs of inventory management and increasing speed of delivery.

E-commerce in China has also seen the influx of cutting-edge technologies with VR and AR being actively used to enhance the shopping experience. On Single's Day in 2016, Alibaba debuted its Buy+ virtual shopping technology, in which shoppers with a VR headset were able to browse products and watch virtual models on a catwalk. Yihaodian, another leading e-commerce platform, launched virtual 3D stores where consumers could only see, visit, and shop through the Yihaodian Virtual Store App while being physically at one of the 1,000 locations and looking at the products via augmented reality.

FIGURE 33

RETAIL SALES (2012 US$ PPP) IN CHINA GREW AT AN ASTOUNDING RATE OVER 2001-2016

PERCENTAGE

- US: 2.7
- CHINA: 12.3
- HONG KONG: 4.8
- INDIA: 7.1
- INDONESIA: 4.7
- MALAYSIA: 7.5
- PHILIPPINES: 5.9
- SOUTH KOREA: 1.9
- TAIWAN: 2.9
- THAILAND: 6.3
- VIETNAM: 9.3

Note: Figures for India, Indonesia, the Philippines, and Thailand; 2015 figure for Vietnam; and 2016 figures for all countries are estimates by Oxford Economics.

GLOBAL CMOS IN A DIVERSE, DYNAMIC REGION

Asia is a very important market, marked by incredible contrasts in business environments, cultures, and levels of development. However, almost all Asian countries are linked by their dramatic economic growth, giving rise to both homegrown companies and global companies seeking to tap in and grab their own piece of the pie.

Those who are successful in the region take a two-pronged approach. First, they localize heavily while still maintaining global markers. Burger King, who saw their sales growing faster in Asia[11] in 2016 than anywhere else in the world, is always adjusting their local approaches. Axel Schwan of Burger King says it's always important for global marketing teams to do their research. "*Test a local approach and a global approach. If your local approach does better, perfect. If there are countries out there that would like to do something differently, we are always open to adjusting our global standards,*" Schwan says. "*I think execution always matters in our industry, but it matters even more when you think about the global role. Then it's about making sure your standards improve the relevance of the brand for different guests around the world."*

The Four Seasons has about 40 hotels and resorts in Asia. Peter Nowlan of Four Seasons Hotels and Resorts says that while one does need to adhere to a central framework for measurement, the digital and social teams need to be able to connect to the local community. *"I think many marketers still try to approach the digital and social world too centrally,"* he explains. *"I believe that you centralize a brand belief and a principle for the framework and you centralize measurement, so you don't keep score differently. Then you decentralize the local connection and community and decision making as much as possible."*

KEEP BRAND RELEVANCE AND IDENTITY CONSISTENT

Riding on the back of the localization/centralization balance, there is also a need for brands to keep their identities consistent across such a broad range of markets and consumer needs, while also maintaining their relevance in each market. The most successful global companies ensure that their identity remains consistent across the board, no matter the localization techniques. There are many different ways to achieve this balance that differ depending on industry. *"This restaurant category is incredibly relevant—and it will probably remain relevant for the next 600 years—but managing consistency and speed of service is very critical,"* says Axel Schwan of Burger King. *"Globally, you need to make sure that the brand consistency is there for the long term. We need to speak with one voice to our guests all around the world, while also remaining locally relevant."* Schwan continues:

Finding this critical balance is definitely one of our key goals as a global team, which means that we need to communicate very, very well. We need to be close to each market so that we can share messages, but also listen to feedback. That is extremely important because whatever we establish—be it our image guidelines, the way we build our restaurants and kitchens, our advertising, or our uniforms—I think we need to truly understand local needs in order to develop the right global standards.

For companies dealing in financial services, they also have to be aware that their consumers are constantly moving, and therefore that consistency across not only Asia but the world is doubly important. *"We know that, as a global*

CASE STUDY

MARS snackfood USA 年年得福

1 **BACKGROUND:** Mars' Dove Chocolate is the number one chocolate brand in China. Their marketing usually targets young, independent women, and they recently decided to switch gears with their 2017 Chinese New Year campaign. With a short, five minute film that chronicles the relationship between mother and daughter, the chocolate giant aimed to drive growth in volume and penetration for the brand by appealing to a broader audience. The driving force behind the campaign was insights which revealed a growing emotional disconnect within families as Chinese people struggle to show emotion and affection, especially to their parents. This case study highlights the importance of adapting to the local market, highlighting the major themes of family and togetherness to celebrate China's biggest holiday.

2 **PROCESS:** A five minute piece of video content was filmed for the campaign. Thomas Delabriere, the VP of Marketing for Mars China said, "This Chinese New Year, Dove wants to be the most talked about campaign for a spot that really touches people's hearts." In the video, their family greeting, "Nian Nian De Fu" (年年得福), has a dual meaning of both "Good Fortune Every Year" and "Dove Every Year." The box of Dove chocolates, which contained all of the mother and daughter's calligraphy over the years, it not only deeply connected to the brand and "Nian nian De Fu," but also worked to create a connection between Chinese New Year blessings with chocolate.

3 **RESULTS:** The campaign's overarching goal was to tell the story of everyone in China, highlighting the importance of family and love, and how it lingers no matter the distance between family as life carries us away from our parents. Dove wanted to touch upon this nerve of their Chinese audience, and remind them that there's always someone that loves you back home. The video struck a chord with the Chinese audience, and within the first month of the video's release it received 27 million views.

company, our consumers are global consumers. They travel all the time. They cross continents and borders. It's important for us to show up as one company, as opposed to being different from country to country," says Raja Rajamannar of Mastercard. *"The consistency is very important. Plus, we also operate under a highly regulated environment. To make sure that what we're doing in one country is not going to land us in a regulatory situation in some other country, we have to be very thoughtful on how we integrate ourselves globally as one. That has been one of the significant areas of our focus."*

However, it is tricky to ensure that the global brand identity and the local story can come together in a meaningful way for consumers. *"What's fascinating is, in the [hospitality and tourism] industry everyone is now scrambling to be locally relevant, and this is what Four Seasons has been about right from the beginning. It is our DNA,"* says Peter Nowlan of Four Seasons Hotels and Resorts. *"The challenge is about finding the right story to tell broadly across markets while elevating the unique features and character of each property across our portfolio."*

PUT THE RIGHT PEOPLE IN PLACE

In addition to localizing brand identity and products, the importance of putting the right leadership in place and ensuring that proper training happens cannot be overstated. A lot of planning happens at the global level, and then it is up to the leadership in local markets to apply global strategies at the local level. Long gone are the days where the only senior management from global companies on the ground in Asia were automatically going to be Westerners. Forward-thinking companies treat countries in Asia as key markets and ensure the right people are in place who truly understand the nuances of the market. *"We've identified key markets for us,"* says David Timm of Pizza Hut. *"We're accelerating learning, putting people with new skills in place, and prioritizing management time. All that is designed to build a repeatable model that we can then execute through other markets."*

Colgate-Palmolive has identified their so-called lead markets, or must-win markets, around the world, where they believe they have to make dramatic changes in e-commerce and digital. *"We have identified leaders in each of these markets who are responsible for this transformation. We have these leaders in about 70 percent of these markets, so it's still not 100 percent there. These leaders are in constant communication with the small team, and there is a very transparent process in place for sharing best practices and resources,"* explains Mukul Deoras of Colgate-Palmolive. *"We have attempted to build a set of leaders who are tasked with driving this change in various places. It is extremely important that these change leaders are passionate about the change because that's how change happens. Change doesn't happen by just sharing best practices and telling people what to do. It is about inspiration. There has to be somebody who's passionate to jumpstart the change."*

UNDERSTAND THE RESOURCES AT HAND

In a very digitally savvy region like Asia, an organization must be able to transform and innovate quickly on the local level, which means building up capabilities in regional or local teams is crucial for success. Andrew Clarke of Mars talks about how important it is to be sensible and methodical about where they have the right resources and capabilities in local markets. *"There are, of course, certain markets that are more digitally mature. China is much further ahead in many ways, particularly when we look at the path to purchase all the way through the consumer journey,"* says Clarke. *"There are tech partners we can partner with and we can really pioneer our own capabilities and drive the agenda faster to test and learn and scale it elsewhere. It's a combination of global, local, and then understanding where we got that digital maturity to test and learn and then scale. It's very exciting."* Mars also runs a China Digital Innovation Center, which reports to the Chief Digital Demand Officer and is concentrating on putting investments in place that show they are dedicated to the region for the long haul.

Colgate-Palmolive is also expanding and localizing its digital capabilities by partnering with Alibaba to launch a brand directly on the e-commerce platform. *"They [the China team] have done a couple of really interesting things. They have launched some new products through e-commerce,"* says Mukul Deoras of Colgate-Palmolive. *"It is a completely different mindset altogether, because now in markets like China you can create a brand with scale through e-commerce."* Deoras emphasizes:

It is important to create some centers of excellence within the organization. The Hill's business; the China business, US business, and LATAM are building best practices. For example, Latin America excels in creating an always-on brand content strategy. The Hill's business is more about creating an impactful consumer engagement strategy and a transaction toward e-commerce. The US center of excellence is focused on data, analytics, influencers, and making sure that we are using social listening as a key driver toward driving brand engagement. China is again about e-commerce, and we're partnering with e-commerce players like Alibaba and driving dramatic engagement and business conversion there.

APPLY LOCAL SUCCESS ON A GLOBAL SCALE

In addition to taking learnings from the central or global headquarters and applying those in the local markets, it's also important that things learned from successful marketing efforts in local markets are brought back to the central office, and perhaps disseminated to other markets in hopes of being successful there too. *"When I think about that [balancing global and local markets], it's an advantage,"* says Jennifer Breithaupt of Citi. She continues:

You have people who are pacing along with different technology and different tools and channels and solutions in different ways, so we can learn from one another. For us, some folks are out ahead of the US doing things and learning and changing and evolving faster. Then, there are things that we're doing in the US that can be exported globally. For us being a global brand, it's a competitive advantage when you think about where we're testing and learning and evolving around the globe. We are always asking, 'How can we do this differently? Or better, here or there?' in different regions and markets around the world.

Peter Nowlan of Four Seasons Hotels and Resorts echoes this sentiment, pointing out that he views each Four Seasons Hotel around the world as its own mini-innovation lab to test and learn. *"The advantage I have is more than 100 labs where we can try things and can see immediate results. We look at what's happening in each region each month, and we talk about what worked and what didn't work which helps inform our decision making going forward,"* says Nowlan.

One way to ensure that success stories from local and regional markets are shared with the global leadership is to make face time a priority between the CMO and global leads. *"I've started having bi-weekly meetings with all of the global leads. Every fortnight, we all come together on a conference call. And every other month, we meet in person,"* explains Raja Rajamannar of Mastercard. *"The whole idea is for each person to share what they are doing, and then for me and the other global team members to see if there is an opportunity to take one brilliant idea, say, for example, digital edge in Asia, into other places. Success transfer is one big thing."*

Marketers from GSK's global teams meet up in a similar fashion to share learnings and as a result, they were able to take the global campaign and tweak it so it resonated with local markets. *"We have a process where we meet on a regular basis through what we call CGTs, or category growth teams. The marketing people from the local markets and our global category teams get together and we share best practices and learnings,"* says Theresa Agnew of GSK Consumer Healthcare. She explains further:

For instance, on Tums, we developed a campaign. We call it the 'Food Fight Campaign' where the person fights with their food that's causing heartburn and then Tums provides fast relief and then you're friends with your food again. This is a campaign that was done in one market first and then spread globally. We use different food depending on the cultural nuances of different countries. We were able to use food that is popular in Latin America, food that made sense in Asia, and also specific food in the US.

Thirty years ago, what worked in the Chinese market and what worked in the US were completely different things. In today's increasingly connected world, the once massive differences between regions are starting to melt away. There are still cultural nuances to take into account when applying global strategies to local markets, but digital is starting closing those gap.

YOU CAN'T MOVE WHAT YOU CAN'T MEASURE

THE IMPORTANCE OF MEASUREMENT

The importance of measurement in the wake of digital transformation cannot be overstated. Mukul Deoras of Colgate-Palmolive asserts, *"If you cannot measure, you cannot change, it's that simple."* From finding the right KPIs, to tracking a campaign's success, to setting up a framework for measuring agency performance, it is impossible to improve without having some concrete data to analyze what's working and what's not.

For example, Samsung works at leveraging both qualitative and quantitative data to inform their marketing decisions. *"We recognize the importance of evaluating our marketing results based on sales or brand value, but we also take a quantitative approach to measuring the performance of our individual marketing efforts,"* says YH

Lee of Samsung. *"Accordingly, the importance of insight-driven marketing activities is increasing."* That being said, there are a significant number of roadblocks that CMOs can face when putting a measurement framework in place.

The rise of programmatic in the media landscape has opened up a Pandora's box of transparency and fraud issues. Evaluating agency partners can be difficult if trust and transparent practices are not established early on in the relationship. The effort to infuse a culture of setting KPIs and executing against them needs to be a top-down effort.

Peter Nowlan of Four Seasons Hotels and Resorts points out that one of the central tenants of the hospitality business—staying attuned to the guests' needs— all starts from setting and tracking the right metrics. *"Having a common point of view and being really guest-centric to what guests want has been the guiding light for the business,"* he says. *"We're doing a lot on metrics and tracking. We've embedded this into the DNA of our organization. Each of us actually. My team all sits with our KPIs on our desks."*

THE CHALLENGES OF MEASUREMENT IN THE DIGITAL AGE

In the wake of digital transformation, traditional metrics for measuring business success like profits, customer satisfaction, and inventory turns might not capture the ROI of all the different digital initiatives across an organization. For a CMO trying to prove marketing's value to an organization, having the right measurement metrics to show the outcomes of their campaigns is very important.

"We focus on developing the right mix of what I call 'metrics and magic' in individuals. Our business is an image business—one you need to have a 'feel' for. But you should be able to ground your recommendations in things like return on investment, research, customer awareness, and penetration metrics," says Syl Saller of Diageo. *"For example, we use Link Optimiser to shape our creative work. It brings the consumer voice into our discussions, and we use it as an aide to judgment rather than a pass/fail test."*

There are many different levels at which digital KPIs can be set and measured.

On an organization-wide macro level, it is important to track the digitization of existing business models, including supply chain, customer service, operations, and marketing. On the micro marketing level, measuring the success of each channel on the consumer journey, as well as assessing individual campaigns, relies on having their own metrics to know what is working and what isn't. One company that has made significant strides in setting up these types of KPIs is Mastercard.

"We plunged headlong into digital and we built the Priceless Engine, which is a digital marketing engine, and we have now rolled it out to all the continents," says Raja Rajamannar of Mastercard. *"Now it's becoming more and more integral to our way of doing business. This has been working very well for us. So much so, our effectiveness levels have been anywhere between two and eight times that of an equivalent regular campaign done the traditional way. This engine is something which has become a huge competitive advantage for us, and driving a lot of efficiency and efficacy."*

The Priceless Engine, an initiative first rolled out in APAC, leveraged the finance giant's analytic capabilities to help its partners understand consumer sentiment and trends based on social conversations, track transactions and engagement on campaigns, create and share content across borders to increase scale, and analyze data quickly to make adjustments in real time.

THE PROGRAMMATIC BLACK BOX

One of the biggest trends in the marketing and advertising industry over the past decade has been the rise of programmatic media buying. This wave of digitization in the media world, where algorithms are largely responsible for buying and placing media in real-time, has led to an industry-wide discussion about measurement revolving around one of the biggest pain points in measuring digital activities: transparency.

Programmatic has become a bit of a buzzword in recent years. There are several different definitions out there, adding to the cloud of confusion around this relatively new way of media buying. It is important to understand what programmatic is and how it works before a meaningful discussion can be had on how to measure it. On the most basic level, programmatic ad buying is the

CASE STUDY

mastercard. PRICELESS

1 **BACKGROUND:** Not many marketing campaigns span two decades, that's just one of the things that makes Mastercard's Priceless campaign one of the marketing industry's biggest success stories. By tapping into the universal truth that experiences matter more than things, Mastercard has been able to bring this campaign into the digital age while staying true to their brand's DNA. Priceless has run in 54 languages in 113 countries to date, and one of the biggest factors in driving its success has been setting and executing against specific KPIs that have allowed Mastercard's marketing team to prove that this campaign has been linked to business success throughout the years, as well as evaluating internal processes and external partnerships to always stay on top of best practice.

2 **PROCESS:** In the very first Priceless commercial, a father takes his son to a baseball game and pays for a hot dog and a drink, but the conversation between the two is priceless and the tagline is "There are some things money can't buy. For everything else, there's MasterCard." In the past 20 years, the concept has expanded into several pillars, including Priceless Cities, Priceless Surprises, Priceless Causes, and Priceless Specials, but the core concept driving the campaign has remained the same. With the onset of digital transformation, the finance giant has learned how to leverage their massive wealth of consumer data to give consumers what they actually want—experiences. Mastercard leverages an immense network of global partners, including agencies, technology vendors, and other companies in the financial and hospitality sectors to make Priceless more than just a marketing campaign, but to integrate it into their consumers' daily lives—connecting with them across several digital touchpoints.

3 **RESULTS:** Mastercard's CMO Raja Rajamannar attributed Priceless' success largely to measuring its impact and adjusting the campaign's objectives to meet business targets. "There are marketing KPIs and there are business metrics. The two cannot be mutually exclusive. Marketers need to clearly connect the dots and demonstrate how campaigns are contributing to business success. By consistently demonstrating this value, we've been able to secure continued investment, enabling the 'Priceless' platform to continue year after year." The success is also tied to the continuous evaluation of their external partnerships. In 2014, Mastercard set out to become the number one player in the digital payments space, forming the "Priceless Engine" after a review of their digital agency model in the region. The platform allows Mastercard to track trends and tailor offers to consumers, bringing Priceless to life in real-time.

automated purchase of digital ad inventory in real time, based on audience rather than platform.

Traditionally, media is purchased based on the platform that the publisher offers. With programmatic ad buying, advertisers are able to target only the specific audience they are trying to reach, using algorithms to optimize campaigns based on several factors garnered from real-time data. That means that instead of reaching every reader of a website, an advertiser can reach only women between the ages of 25-35 who own a cat, for example. Many people use the term real-time bidding (RTB) interchangeably with programmatic when in reality, RTB is only one type of programmatic buying. An RTB transaction takes place in milliseconds, beginning when a consumer clicks a website link and ending before the page even loads. Communication between the publisher's ad servers and all the intermediaries—the demand-side platforms (DSPs), supply-side platforms (SSPs), and data management platforms (DMPs)—happens in a fraction of a second, and bids are placed to determine which ad will be displayed.

Real-time bidding is just one type of programmatic transaction. It is most often used in the most basic type of market, the open exchange. In an open exchange, there is no relationship between the publisher and the advertiser. Any participating buyer can access the inventory, and advertisers are usually unaware what publisher's site their ad is being displayed on. The second type of programmatic is called invitation-only auction, or private marketplace (PMP). The inventory in PMP is more premium than on the open exchange, and only invited brands can buy impressions. However, the bidding is still done by RTB to ensure that the highest bidder still wins the impression.

Next on the ladder is the unreserved fixed-rate exchange, or the preferred deal model. This inventory has a pre-negotiated fixed price, but no guaranteed volume.

The last major bucket of programmatic is the automated guaranteed, or programmatic premium model. This type of transaction uses reserved inventory and a fixed price between the buyer and seller. It resembles a traditional digital buy, except the RFP and campaign tracking process is automated.

One major challenge for brands when adopting a programmatic media strategy is the difference between diverse markets. Take China and the US, for example.

FIGURE 34

THE LIFE OF A PROGRAMMATIC
RTB AD IMPRESSION

IN A FRACTION OF A SECOND

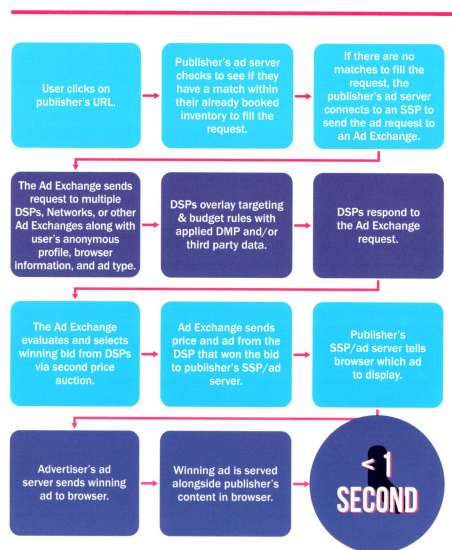

User clicks on publisher's URL.

Publisher's ad server checks to see if they have a match within their already booked inventory to fill the request.

If there are no matches to fill the request, the publisher's ad server connects to an SSP to send the ad request to an Ad Exchange.

The Ad Exchange sends request to multiple DSPs, Networks, or other Ad Exchanges along with user's anonymous profile, browser information, and ad type.

DSPs overlay targeting & budget rules with applied DMP and/or third party data.

DSPs respond to the Ad Exchange request.

The Ad Exchange evaluates and selects winning bid from DSPs via second price auction.

Ad Exchange sends price and ad from the DSP that won the bid to publisher's SSP/ad server.

Publisher's SSP/ad server tells browser which ad to display.

Advertiser's ad server sends winning ad to browser.

Winning ad is served alongside publisher's content in browser.

<1 SECOND

There are several factors that contribute to the unique nature of programmatic advertising in China. First, the digital ecosystem as a whole is radically different, as the major players of the Western world such as Facebook, Google, YouTube, and Yahoo rarely operate in China, if at all. As was mentioned in Chapter 7, BAT are the major programmatic players in China. In addition, the lack of good third party data and the limitations on the exchange of information lead to even bigger transparency issues than are found in other markets.

The biggest challenge CMOs face when approaching programmatic media is transparency, or a lack thereof. Raja Rajamannar of Mastercard revealed that he was surprised at the lack of transparency when he first started learning about programmatic. *"A few years back, I actually went to one of the DSPs; I sat with them and tried to understand everything end to end, including what is inside the black box. I realized that the process has holes you can drive trucks through. But unless you do those kinds of trainings, it looks like it's just a black box and you trust the black box blindly and go with it,"* he says.

AD FRAUD - PROBLEMS AND SOLUTIONS

So what is the so-called programmatic black box? Major complaints from advertisers include the fact that, for the most part, whoever is buying the inventory has no control over the sites that their ads are being displayed on. Additionally, the advertiser has no way of knowing what type of content their ad ran alongside, or if a human even saw the ad. There are several different types of ad fraud in the programmatic world, and staying on top of these issues is crucial to leveraging this technology while facing problems inherent in the system. In 2014, at the Ad Age Data Conference,[1] Kraft announced that they would reject between 75–85 percent of digital impressions bought in real-time bidding marketplaces due to fraud concerns.

As the buying and selling of ad inventory becomes more automated, the lack of human oversight means that there are more opportunities for fraud to gain a foothold. The most common type of fraud is the use of a non-human bot that registers impressions or clicks on ads. In some cases, there is little incentive on both the side of the buyer and the side of the seller to detect and weed out this type of fraud. It allows the operations team to look like they are buying a great deal of traffic for very cheap, and at the same time, the publishers are able to increase audience and insure a steady revenue stream. The biggest issue of bot traffic is that advertisers think that they are meeting their campaign KPIs when in fact, an actual human has never seen or clicked on their ad.

There are also many types of human ad fraud that have nothing to do with bots. These include things like click farms, where real people are paid to click on ads and sometimes even fill out forms, resulting in worthless impressions and conversions. There are other things like domain spoofing, site bundling, and arbitrage, which involve the intentional misrepresentation of inventory or reselling inventory for a fraction of the cost paid for it.

Many leading brands are taking steps to battle fraud. According to MediaRadar estimates for 2017,[2] P&G ran ads on 978 sites between January and May, which is a 33 percent decrease from the 1,459 sites P&G ran ads on during the same period last year. At the same time, Unilever had ads on 540 sites between January and May, an 11 percent decrease from 606 sites they ran ads on during the same period in 2016. A separate survey of 35 multinational marketers from the WFA revealed that 55 percent of advertisers are limiting the number of ads they buy on open ad exchanges, while 89 percent already limit or plan to limit spending in ad networks that are not independently verified.

As the programmatic marketplace has matured, many different types of pre- and post-bid anti-fraud solutions have come onto the marketplace. One of the best protections is to consider the highest level of buying, and stay off the open exchanges. However, for those who don't buy programmatic directly, there are ad verification vendors that can analyze campaign data, showing things like invalid impressions and viewability metrics.

Perhaps the best protection against fraud is education; knowing what type of data is necessary to minimize fraud and make sure that media spends are working as hard as they possibly can. Many advertisers find themselves woefully uneducated in the realm of media buying (both traditional and programmatic); since they always had a media partner to take care of this part of the marketing mix, why would they need to understand how it works? This knowledge gap on the marketers' side led to another type of transparency issue that rocked the media world in early 2017—transparency issues with media agencies themselves.

FIGURE 35

AD FRAUD -
PROBLEMS & SOLUTIONS

While no **ONE KNOWS FOR CERTAIN** exactly what percentage of impressions **ARE FRAUDULENT,** the estimates reach as high as **40%**

THE ASSOCIATION OF NATIONAL ADVERTISERS (ANA)

Did a **60 DAY** study to gauge the severity of fraud in **181 CAMPAIGNS** among **36** of their members, including **JNJ, Walmart,** and **Kimberly-Clark**

They found that bots accounted for **23%** of video impressions **&** **11%** of display ads

Which they projected would account for **$6.3 BILLION** in **LOSSES** in **2015** alone.

TRANSPARENCY AND AGENCY PARTNERS

The focus on non-transparent practices among media agencies really began in 2012, when 28 percent of respondents to an Association of National Advertisers (ANA) member survey indicated awareness of media rebate practice in the US. In response, the ANA conducted a report to do a deep-dive investigation into these practices in 2016. The report sent shockwaves through the advertising industry, finding that "cash rebates" and other "non-transparent practices" are, in fact, pervasive in the US media buying ecosystem. Even though the report didn't name specific agency groups or media vendors due to its confidential nature, it left an air of suspicion between partners. One of the most alarming aspects of the report didn't have anything to do with the actual non-transparent practices, but rather the fact that many advertisers were unaware of the details in the agency contracts that addressed transparency.

FIGURE 36

HOW SHOULD CMOS RESPOND?

 1 CHANGE CONTRACTS IMMEDIATELY

Marketers will have no legal standing in this debate, unless the wording in their contracts with their agencies protects them from these kinds of issues. Most don't.

2 REPORT REBATES REGULARLY

Rebates are not going away, but the best agencies are proactively reporting these on a quarterly basis to their clients, so that media channel decisions can be mutually made on what will most effectively reach the consumer.

3 AUDIT AGENCIES ANNUALLY

A simple onsite financial audit by a third party is crucial to make sure agencies are accountable and fulfilling their legal commitments. It makes no sense for one company to give another $10m, $50m, or $100m and not expect some independent oversight on how it was invested.

Marketers have to take responsibility for some of the transparency issues facing the industry today. This responsibility comes in the form of knowing (or in this case, not knowing) what is in their own agency contracts. Many client-agency contracts have not been reviewed or updated in ten years. The ecosystem is fragmented and complicated as the media industry is changing every day, and it can be difficult to keep up with rapid changes in technology. However, the ANA report makes it evident that if the marketers don't stay informed, some agencies will be right there to take advantage of their ignorance.

HOW ARE CMOS EVALUATING AGENCY PARTNERS?

The transparency issues tie into one of the most important foundations between a CMO and their agency partners: trust. Trust between two partners is essential for any relationship to be successful. However, there is something to be said about the old adage *trust, but verify*. KPIs and measurement standards shouldn't only be applied to digital initiatives and campaigns in the modern marketing world.

The best client-agency relationships in the world have a robust evaluation framework in place to ensure mutual success, and that the goals of the partnership are being met. Sadly, one of the most neglected areas of managing marketing partners is a structured, multiway, actionable evaluation system. The world's best marketers also routinely have the world's best agency evaluation frameworks—taking this approach very seriously, and setting KPIs as part of an agency incentive. Only by making sure agencies have "skin in the game" can you truly align both organizations behind the same mutual goal.

There are four key areas to consider when developing an agency evaluation framework. The first is to appoint key players. The evaluation should be reflective of those people in the client organization who work with the agency on a regular basis. Closely involving senior management on both the client and agency side is necessary to ensure that the stakeholders ultimately accountable for the relationship are active participants in the formal evaluation. The second is a strong two-way channel of communication. The agency should be actively involved in the process upfront and throughout. Conducting a 360-degree review allows the agency to evaluate the client as well, resulting in improved productivity of the relationship. The best advertising results from effective collaboration between the two sides. The identification of best practices, problems,

> "It's an incredible job, driving the efficiency in this company and making sure that the dollars are being spent in the right places. We're getting out the costs where we don't need them. It starts with the customer and understanding 'what does the customer need' and making sure we are building toward that and not having these expensive solutions that customers don't need and making sure we're always investing where the puck is going."
>
> **MEREDITH VERDONE**
> *Bank of America*

and solutions on the client side of the relationship can benefit productivity just as it can on the agency side.

The third important element is to align on a clear direction from the onset. Effective evaluations do not simply give the agency a grade; rather, they spell out the particular good and bad performance areas with enough detail that the client and agency can effectively diagnose and act. Communicating a clear and actionable message with focus is crucial to giving direction to the agency that is consistent across the client team, rather than giving a laundry list of competing or conflicting issues. The evaluation should cover all areas of significant agency activity on behalf of the client.

The last important component is to drive more accountability. In order for the performance evaluation to be acted upon, the marketer must go beyond providing a report card. Effective evaluations result in an agreed-upon plan of action that the agency and client follow up on with designated steps, timing, and accountability. The goals set in taking steps forward must be realistic and

FIGURE 37

AGENCY EVALUATION CRITERIA

CREATIVE AGENCIES

 ADVERTISER
Sales
(Sales Index)
Market Share Growth
Growth by Brand

 ADVERTISING
Brand Health
Equity Measures
Ad Awareness
Ad Recall
Pre-tests
Link Results

 AGENCY
Annual Evaluation
Half Year Evaluations

MEDIA AGENCIES

 ADVERTISER
Sales
(Sales Index)
Market Share Growth
Growth by Brand

ADVERTISING
Advertising Awareness
Advertising Recall

 AGENCY
Annual Evaluation
Half Year Evaluations
Media Efficiency Audits
Media Effectiveness Audits
Media Financial Audits
Media Process Audits

DIGITAL AGENCIES

 ADVERTISER
Sales
(Sales Index)
Market Share Growth
Growth by Brand

 ADVERTISING
Advertising Awareness
Advertising Recall

 AGENCY
Annual Evaluation
Half Year Evaluations
Digital KPIs

EVENT AGENCIES

 ADVERTISER
Sales
(Sales Index)
Market Share Growth
Growth by Brand

 ADVERTISING
Advertising Awareness
Advertising Recall

AGENCY
Annual Evaluation
Half Year Evaluations
Event Metrics
Event Performance

SOCIAL AGENCIES

 ADVERTISER
Sales
(Sales Index)
Market Share Growth
Growth by Brand

 ADVERTISING
Advertising Awareness
Advertising Recall

 AGENCY
Annual Evaluation
Half Year Evaluations
Social Metrics

achievable. A high level of performance should be expected of the agency, but the client must be realistic about what the agency is expected to accomplish. Setting the right KPIs needs to take the type of agency involved into account. However, regardless of the type of agency, the structure of KPIs should always relate to the performance of the advertiser, the advertising, and the agency. With this in mind, marketers can drive greater consistency and predictability through your KPIs.

FINDING THE RIGHT COMPENSATION MODEL

Agency remuneration is one of the most important factors affecting the client-agency relationship, yet for many in the C-suite it is one of the least understood. Today's remuneration model options are much more varied and complicated than in the previous century when media commissions prevailed. Having a fundamental understanding of agency cost drivers and the impact that fee agreements can have on agency motivation, capacity, and capability is crucial to being able to effectively negotiate and manage agency relationships, regardless of the method of remuneration selected or the type of agency. While there is no silver bullet solution, the best agency remuneration agreements serve both the client and agency. Any remuneration agreement that works to the disadvantage of either party will eventually work to the disadvantage of both parties. An inequitable remuneration agreement will usually result in an unproductive, and potentially contentious, relationship between the client and agency.

There are five major types of compensation models: commission-based, a base fee tied to client media spending; labor-based, a fee based on actual time spent; output-based, fees based on individual project costs; performance-based, a base retainer fee with incentives for achieving mutually agreed KPIs/results; and value-based, fees based on the perceived value of an outcome.

Since the best practice for arriving at the right remuneration model is based on the qualities of fairness, adaptability, simplicity, reward, and predictability, by extension the remuneration model does not necessarily require customization to each of the different agency partners that a marketer engages. In fact, having one consistently applied remuneration model across all partners—in today's world of fragmentation and hyper-specialization—serves to build further efficiency and expertise into the process. That said, certain remuneration methods lend themselves better to certain agencies and services than others, and each company needs to do what is best for both their bottom line and their agency partners.

In early 2017, the ANA released the 17th version of their triennial compensation trends report.[3] The study showed that marketers are seeking to simplify their compensation methods, with a decline in labor-based fees and performance incentives and an increase in value-based remuneration methods.

FIGURE 38

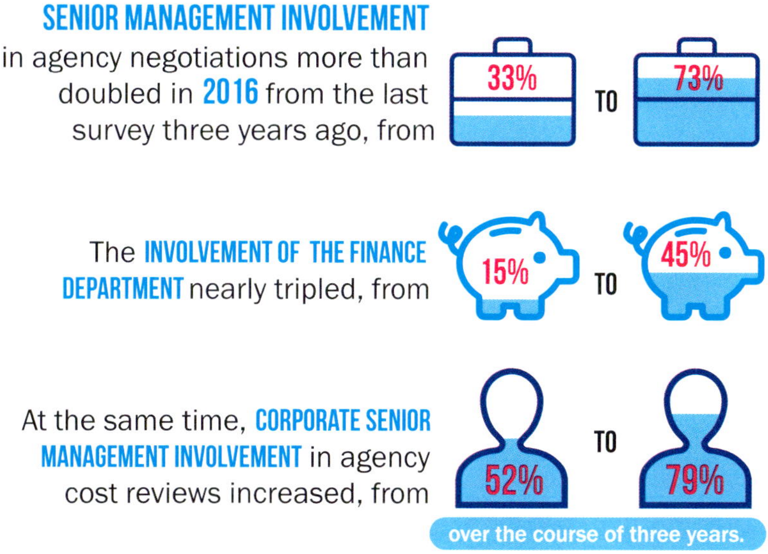

SENIOR MANAGEMENT INVOLVEMENT in agency negotiations more than doubled in **2016** from the last survey three years ago, from 33% TO 73%

The **INVOLVEMENT OF THE FINANCE DEPARTMENT** nearly tripled, from 15% TO 45%

At the same time, **CORPORATE SENIOR MANAGEMENT INVOLVEMENT** in agency cost reviews increased, from 52% TO 79% over the course of three years.

SETTING MARKETING BUDGETS AND PLANNING AGENCY FEES

One of the biggest challenges facing CMOs that ties back to agency evaluation and KPI setting is setting marketing budgets and planning agency fees. *"I think the other core challenge is going to be how you allocate your resources,"* says David Timm of Pizza Hut. He continues:

You know you need to shift more money into conversion and retention. As you shift the money into conversion and retention, which is highly measurable, you're shifting it away from the things that are less measurable. Figuring out what the right balance is and the opportunity costs of moving from, for example, an awareness campaign into optimizing search will be one of the challenges for all marketing departments. We don't have incremental advertising budgets. If you shift a million dollars into conversion and retention it has to come out of what you're currently doing on acquisition. At its simplest, if you're spending an incremental million dollars on search, it's a million dollars less for your TV or other GRPs. It's just about figuring out the balance between all of the different possible channels you've got now and how you shift your resources between them. Not just the media spend but also the people working on it, et cetera. This is our core challenge.

For a CMO, planning where to invest the most of the marketing budget—be it with campaigns, technology, or agency fees—is becoming increasingly difficult, as many senior marketers are under pressure to cut costs. There are also trends in budget planning that recycle every few years, and zero-based budgeting is having its moment in the sun right now. Several of the world's largest markets are using this method right now, including Unilever, Coca-Cola, Nestle, Kraft-Heinz, and others. Zero-based budgeting works by wiping the budget slate clean every year and starting from zero (hence the name), rather than extrapolating on the past years' trends and next year's revenue projections to create a budget.

Meredith Verdone of Bank of America highlights her consumer-centric approach to allocating marketing spends:

It's an incredible job, driving the efficiency in this company and making sure that the dollars are being spent in the right places. We're getting out the costs where we don't need them. It starts with the customer and understanding 'what does the customer need' and making sure we are building toward that and not having these expensive solutions that customers don't need and making sure we're always investing where the puck is going.

Mukul Deoras of Colgate-Palmolive points out that the right digital KPIs are crucial to changing budget discussion in the C-suite:

We're now putting simple measurements templates in place. They might not be 100% accurate, but they are definitely directionally right. How do you measure if what you are doing is right or not, should you do more, should you do less? We all grew up in the share of voice era, and we are very comfortable talking about share of voice because I can ask for more budget if our share of voice is low—so it becomes a very good tool to budget investment. But now, we have to equip people to think a little differently. We have to measure not just input (like share of voice) but also output (like engagement, transaction). We have started creating templates and training people on how to use them. And it's not just training the people who are using them, but the business leaders also need to be brought up to speed. If the business leaders continue to focus only on share of voice, all they will hear about is share of voice. If they don't ask the right questions about digital KPIs and understand the meaning behind those KPIs, then the conversation in business meetings will not change. When the conversations don't change, the behaviors don't change. I think you have to attack this problem from all possible directions.

SETTING KPIS TO DRIVE BUSINESS

Measurement will be a challenge for CMOs as the number of tools available expands and the agency model changes, but it will become even more important in proving marketing's value to the business. *"In very simple terms, we ask the marketing people to connect the dots between marketing KPIs which they know well, and the business metrics that everybody else truly cares for,"* says Raja Rajamannar of Mastercard. In the end, the main goal of measuring both digital marketing activities and agency performance is to prove marketing's value in achieving business goals.

Shell is another company working to standardize KPIs to track the impact on overall business performance. *"One thing I've been working on is creating a measurement framework. A limited number of options that people can choose from in briefings and setting KPIs is so that, at a minimum, we are able to compare campaigns with each other,"* says Linda van Schaik of Shell. *"Before we did that, everyone took the metric for the KPI that they liked themselves, or that looked most impressive. We're trying to standardize the measurement framework. It doesn't mean that it's always the same KPIs year after year, but at least the set is standardized and we're learning more and more which ones are really driving our business."*

CASE STUDY

DIAGEO CATALYST

1 **BACKGROUND:** In order to face this new world of marketing, marketers are being asked to do more with less budget, prove ROI, and find the right blend of effectiveness and efficiency without sacrificing creativity. Diageo created a new digital interface, Catalyst, in an attempt to ensure that their marketing dollars are delivering the best outcomes. Their new platform attempts to help their 1,200 marketers across 55 countries make the best possible strategic decisions, based on real-time data coming from Catalyst.

2 **PROCESS:** Catalyst's functionality is two-fold. First, it puts together data from several different sources to determine the best possible budget for each of Diageo's brands, based on factors like the success of previous marketing programs and potential profits. Second, it analyzes the possible impact of planned activity. Both the short-term and long-term outcomes of marketing activities are analyzed, and the result is recommendations on where to put marketing dollars for each brand across different regions and different channels on a weekly basis. This type of data-driven decision making is becoming increasingly popular among today's marketers, especially in the FMCG vertical. Diageo's goal is to change their marketers' ways of thinking, and ensure that their investments are delivering the best possible outcomes for the business overall, no matter the market.

3 **RESULTS:** In terms of Diageo's media planning partners, who previously did much of the leg work now done by Catalyst, the alcohol giant asserted that it has actually led to a deepening of the partnerships and faster executions. Since the launch of the platform, Diageo has increased the profit gained as a result of marketing activities, as well as increased their teams' effectiveness. This tool is allowing marketers to have instant access to campaign returns, allowing them to better focus marketing spend on more strategic and higher performing campaigns. Catalyst is just one of the tools Diageo has implemented to reduce inefficiencies company-wide, in addition to Zero-Based Budgeting and reducing supply chain waste. Through these initiatives, the company's goal is to deliver over 900 million USD in savings by the end of 2019.

BUILDING A MODERN MARKETING PLAYBOOK

Today's modern marketing organization is very different from the days of the advertising Mad Men. The relatively flat structure of marketing teams in the past doesn't translate to today's reality as more and more functions are being integrated into marketing. The marketers of yesteryear didn't have to worry about social media, consumer insights, data and analytics, digital CRM systems, and connected devices. As long as they were well-versed in the classic consumer purchase funnel, and had one creative and media agency to handle campaigns, they would be fine. Whereas the old funnel ended when a consumer made a purchase, in today's world the marketing and sales funnel has expanded to include new post-purchase steps. The marketing function is now responsible for more of the consumer journey than ever before, and in order to keep up with these new responsibilities, there needs to be major changes to the way marketing teams are structured and how they fit into the wider organizational structure.

FIGURE 39

THE EVOLUTION OF THE MARKETING FUNNEL

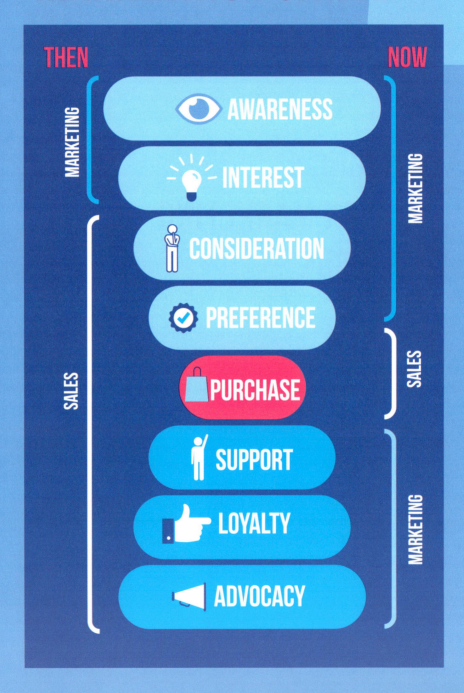

THEN

NOW

MARKETING

AWARENESS

INTEREST

CONSIDERATION

PREFERENCE

PURCHASE

SUPPORT

LOYALTY

ADVOCACY

SALES

MARKETING

SALES

MARKETING

The modern marketing playbook starts with a change in mindset. Digital transformation across an organization requires a top-down initiative to get teams excited about changing long-standing processes—which can sometimes seem like a daunting task. It also requires a long-term investment in education and talent, both of which are critical to make sure that the team is digitally savvy. Most importantly, the traditional silos of large organizations need to be broken down. It can no longer be that marketing, sales, IT, and human resources (HR) operate completely separately from one another. To affect real digital transformation, all departments need to be working together to support the organization's business goals.

BATTLING THE LEGACY DISEASE

Perhaps one of the biggest obstacles for companies, especially older companies that are well-established in markets all over the world, is to be slowed down by the so-called "legacy disease." In several of R3's recent CMO roundtable events, the attendees have mentioned that their organizations are dealing with this disease, symptoms of which include the inability to change quickly due to entrenched and outdated processes, working behind the trend curve, and being laden down by layers of bureaucracy.

As evident by the first-hand accounts of the CMOs interviewed for this book, today's work environment is becoming more spontaneous, virtual, and hyper-connected. Learning is also becoming more KPI-driven and measurable, and organizations that take an outdated approach to training and upskilling their employees will lag behind companies taking a forward-thinking, digital-first approach. In order to keep up, CMOs need to infuse new ways of learning and problem solving into the everyday workflow of their teams. This could include anything from changing the entire way their companies approach problem solving, to balancing the acquisition of new talent with building the capabilities of current employees in order to make the entire company Future Fit. The key is being able to balance transformation with core brand values so that the company doesn't lose its differentiating factor.

For Mastercard, one step on their digital transformation journey was making subtle changes to their branding. For such a well-established legacy company, the challenge was significant. Their goal was to become digital-first, while not sacrificing the brand equity that took 45 years to build. Their branding team embarked on nearly two and half years of research and design to update their branding for a digital world. They had to retain the colors and the globally recognizable interlocking circles, but they made subtle adjustments to make the logo more contemporary and usable across all digital platforms.

"Where digital is the future, it [the logo] is more optimized for digital viewership. Likewise, we wanted to see if consumers recognized that logo without the name Mastercard, and it was a stunning 84 percent. We said, 'Okay, we got something,'" says Raja Rajamannar of Mastercard. He continues:

Down the line, I clearly envision an opportunity for us where we can completely take the name away, but we didn't want to do it on day one. What we said is, 'Let's pull Mastercard from within the circle, or within those interlocking circles and put it below.' That was a huge transformation for us from a pure branding perspective, and the consumer reaction was that it was more modern, contemporary, exciting, youthful, and a future-proof, digitally savvy, and upscale brand logo.

One company that has beat the legacy disease is GE. Now one of the shining stars of organizational digital transformation, this mindset starts with their CMO, Linda Boff, whose goal is to operate like a 125-year-old start-up company. This mindset has been key to how Boff's team, and GE as a whole, approached the future. *"I think it's some of what we're talking about,"* says Boff. *"I think it's every single day, every morning, waking up, fighting for relevance, fighting for modernity, never taking it for granted. Never, never, never say it's enough. It is the spirit of the whole company. It's this fight for relevance and the examples are littered all around us."*

CHANGING THE DIALOGUE

To break free from the shackles of the old way of doing things, CMOs and their teams have to think outside the box, and have the bravery to break rules (within reason) when doing so could potentially lead to a new, improved solution or new way of approaching a problem. This means taking a hard look at the way the world is developing and moving, as well as asking the hard questions about how these new developments relate to a CMO's company and the way they're reaching out to consumers. *"We have to be excellent observers. It must be constant. We must be very inquisitive. Always ask why. In every industry, there are unwritten rules, and these days we have to be willing to break some rules to be truly disruptive,"* says Andres Kiger of Converse.

Sometimes, thinking outside the box means going against deeply ingrained instincts. For Diageo, expanding their portfolio meant tapping into a growing craft alcohol movement (and a shift toward consumers drinking less alcohol). But instead of trying to one-up these smaller companies, or drive them out of business, Diageo decided to invest in them.

"In the UK, there are 300 gin and whiskey distilleries, and 1,500 in the States. So, picture the conversation… We're asking for a whole bunch of money to invest in brands that could compete with us. And, oh by the way, people are drinking less, so we also want to invest in non-alcoholic start-ups too," says Syl Saller of Diageo. Saller emphasizes this point about working with start-ups early on:

Rather than see craft brands as a threat, we want to partner with the best. We keep them entrepreneurial and outside of our system—but we have the first right to buy them when they get to scale. In this way we've created the world's first spirits accelerator through distill ventures. In the old days, investing in potential competitors sounded crazy. But we've learned you have to be where the consumer is. So what sounds like a crazy idea, at first, is actually a brave idea and it becomes the new normal.

Part of being brave is reaching out to and interacting with consumers, engaging with them directly, listening to their ideas, and reacting to them. While this doesn't mean making major changes in branding every time someone sends a tweet, it is important to move away from isolation and to make consumers feel like they are involved with and empowered by the brands they love. One example of this new way of thinking is Lenovo's logo redesign. They went to their fans when it was time to redesign their logo, and directly involved them in the process.

"We approached it from an outside-in perspective. Rather than develop it from our internal view point, we went to our fans and users and sought their help in the process," says David Roman of Lenovo. *"It took about the same time to develop as the*

traditional process would have been, and the cost difference was minimal. However, the level of engagement we achieved and the excitement and passion we generated internally and externally was fantastic. People really felt [like] part of the process as we changed our logo and that was very exciting for us."

Starting with the consumer and really understanding their needs is a solid foundation to kick start digital transformation. Challenging organizational norms to make sweeping changes can be an intimidating process for CMOs. Thinking outside the box involves a certain level of risk. What if something doesn't go as planned? What if a new process doesn't work the way you thought it would? It's important not to let these doubts get in the way of meaningful change, because, as Andrew Clarke of Mars points out, digital isn't going away. *"Invest for the future, execute brilliantly, and continue to learn on the journey. That's the set up. That disruption, that challenge, is not going to go away, it's only going to grow,"* says Clarke. *"The way we embrace it is the most important thing. That will mean challenging some orthodoxies and doing things differently and maybe some disruptive business models and some partnerships we've not thought about before."*

SIX STEPS TO HELP GET THE DIGITAL TRANSFORMATION GOING

FIGURE 40

MISSION

1 **START FROM THE CUSTOMER:** Prioritize key customer journeys and digitize end to end.

2 **BREAK YOUR FUNCTIONAL SILOS:** Build a cross-functional team with a clear mandate and digital talent.

GROUND CONTROL

3 **CREATE MEASURABLE TARGETS:** Develop quantitative targets for each team.

4 **TRANSLATE DIGITAL AMBITION INTO RESOURCE ALLOCATIONS AND BUDGETS:** Significantly relocate investments.

BOOSTER

5 **FOCUS ON TALENT:** Infuse new leader into organization; retain existing digital talent.

6 **MAXIMIZE VALUE OF TWO-SPEED IT:** Digitally enable your legacy infrastructure.

LEARN, STUDY, KNOW

The most exciting, and perhaps scariest, part of this new digital age where the power dynamics are in constant flux between traditional giants, digital disruptors, and smaller, more agile companies is the need to break out of your comfort zone. For Theresa Agnew of GSK Consumer Healthcare, she and her team work hard to stay current and attuned to the platforms and technology behind the consumer experience. *"It's not technology for the sake of technology that is new,"* Agnew says, *"but what will make the consumer journey and the consumer experience more frictionless."*

What she and her team do to tackle this challenge is meet with start-up companies in Silicon Valley to learn about and keep abreast of emerging technologies. *"I think that will be one of the biggest challenges in the next few years—making sure that we know what platforms consumers are going to be using and any apps that they're going to have."* Agnew continues:

It will be important to continue to be a learning organization. We have developed so that we are constantly taking in new insights, new technologies, new ways of working. We have done a lot of testing and learning through the years. We try new media platforms and different digital technology. We will continue to have this mindset of wanting to learn and wanting to build new skills. We're very focused on building capability throughout our organization.

In addition to looking to the outside for new information, technology, and trends, learning more about the internal operations of different branches of the company—how their experiences differ from market to market and how different solutions work (or don't)—is just as important to making meaningful change. Shell is actively engaging with their franchises to learn about their experiences, and working to apply those learnings to possible future solutions. *"We have different initiatives going where we join customers or join certain franchises—a fleet manager, for example—to understand their experience throughout the day. What do they do? Where are the bottlenecks?"* says Linda van Schaik of Shell. *"Then we extrapolate the learnings to understand their potential future needs. Then, we work from there, either with partners or internally, to test and learn."*

Another global company with franchises all over the world is Pizza Hut. They also try to arm their franchisees with knowledge gained through testing and learning, so they make the case for transformation armed with concrete data on what will drive business success. *"Testing and improving is important because it's how we build the business case for change with our franchisees. It's not based on what we think, but on what we know,"* says David Timm of Pizza Hut.

BREAK DOWN INTERNAL SILOS

At a recent R3 CMO roundtable, a former Coca-Cola marketing leader identified two major tensions in today's marketing landscape, the first of which is the shift to fragmentation. The challenge is that many marketers have to be in the now and in the future at the same time, which simply isn't feasible for many companies. The second source of tension is that the nature of fragmentation has changed, with both types of choices and sheer number of options that consumers face increasing exponentially.

Essentially, the landscape today is like going from playing checkers to playing chess. The end result is that there are too many internal silos, making it difficult for all the teams to go to market together, impacting both the consumer and the transaction. This has led to a content creation problem, with no connection from team to team. Companies need to shift thinking from going vertically to going horizontally across an organization.

CMOs need to reimagine their definition of integration to go beyond the basic understanding, and shift their focus to the consumer journey, market intelligence, and stakeholder needs. They also need to become "collaboration savvy," knowing when (and when not to) collaborate across teams. Internal integration is hard work—you have to understand your own integration model, disrupt practices internally, and enable drive. Large, legacy companies typically have many departments that are optimized for specialization and efficiency within their own function. However, into today's fast-moving digital environment, this hinders agility and the sharing of often-times crucial information or data across those siloes. The result of these siloes is business leaders who are resistant to change and are territorial in the face of cross-functional collaboration.

In some sense, this is unknown territory. When there are no more defined lines between the functions of an organization, how do leaders align on how responsibilities should be allocated? *"We will become increasingly more dependent on others as an organization, particularly the CIO,"* says Mukul Deoras of Colgate-Palmolive. He continues:

Obviously, our relationship with the R&D [research and development] organization continues to be extremely strong. That's not new. Traditionally there is a strong relationship between marketing and sales. These are two bodies that are joined at the hip, and they have to thrive together. One creates the demand, one services the demand. It is about ensuring mental availability and physical availability of our products together. That servicing of the demand used to happen through the customer. But the entire model is undergoing a change now with customers getting disintermediated, and the boundaries between advertising, media, sales, and promotion start disappearing. We are entering into an unknown territory.

This will be the true challenge for CMOs going forward—deciding where one function ends and the other begins, as well as figuring out which collaborations will drive efficiency versus create unnecessary bottlenecks.

David Timm of Pizza Hut, whose team has seen an incredible series of digital innovations and launches, believes that it is important that digital marketing and traditional marketing fit within a single structure and team in order to function in an environment that is more direct to consumer. He says:

I believe it is important that digital marketing and traditional marketing fit within a single structure and team. It's important because we need real fluidity of budget, and you need to be able to shift your money around depending on what you see day to day. If you're sitting in different functions then people become possessive over their territory and funds… I think the total marketing function needs to be one rather than split up over a number of different departments. We do separate the people who are building the interfaces, either apps or websites, but remain highly connected with them. We need to be joined at the hip. That's quite new for us as we now appreciate that technology is more important that it was historically. We drive sales but we don't have salespeople because we are direct to consumer, who access our stores directly or online.

In order to break down the walls, CMOs and other C-suite executives must take the first step, as change always begins with the examples that leadership sets. This means being enthusiastic about the changes, as well as crafting your own team structures to align with the larger goal of cross-collaboration. Andrew Clarke of Mars has a Chief Digital Demand Officer who reports to him, but leads the Mars digital center of excellence that works across their segments with the purpose of boosting expertise and leveraging their partnerships with tech companies like Facebook, Google, Alibaba, Tencent, and Amazon. *"This is where we tackle some of the common challenges we see, and experiment on behalf of the business in a consistent way. The global team often partners with our segments or a local market to try new approaches before we scale it across the organization,"* says Clarke. He continues:

The same on the customer side, we're seeing e-commerce and digital across a number of the account management relationships. The lines between sales and marketing are blurred when it comes to digital. Basically, when we started this journey two or three years ago, we had a separate e-commerce team, and we had a separate digital team. Increasingly, this is permeating all the way through everybody's role.

Another advantage to breaking down traditional boundaries is joining the data and creative functions together, combining their knowledge and perspectives and hopefully seeing crossover between the two. *"The best marketing people are both brand and digital focused. They understand the combination of art and science that is required—conversion and sales go hand-in-hand with awareness,"* says Maryam Banikarim of Hyatt Hotels. *"There's still room for people to be better and bring those two worlds together. When you have really good insights and those pieces come together, you're able to deliver the best offering for the customer."*

While most global organizations are in the beginning stages of truly breaking down silos and integrating horizontally across internal functions. The marketing team structure of the future has the possibility to look very different if it is truly driven by a consumer-centric strategy. Rather than directives coming top-down from the C-suite based on revenue numbers or past years' budget numbers, the function's goals will start from the bottom up—beginning solely from consumer insights and moving up through the function.

FIGURE 41

THE MARKETING TEAM OF THE FUTURE

LEADERSHIP
CMO+VPs+Directors

MANAGEMENT
Marketing, Project, Event Managers + Producers

STRATEGY
Planning+Creative Leadership

OPTIMIZATION
Performance Analysis + Testing

REACH
Paid, Earned,
Community Management + Email

CONTENT, TOOLS + EXPERIENCES
UX, Dev, Design, Video,
Photo, Audio + Copywriting

CONSUMER INSIGHTS
Monitoring + Segmentation

Marko Z Mueller

BRING IN THE RIGHT TALENT

In the wake of all this digital change, it is tempting for CMOs to pack the benches with a sea of new faces who have digital splashed in bold letters across their resumes. It is true that some fresh talent in the marketing department must be digitally fluent, but it's not enough to just bring in new talent and hope for the best. *I think like any change, if it's disruptive, it's hard work. I think we've recognized that it's not enough to just bring in the right skills set because of the change management component,* says David Timm of Pizza Hut. *"You need to find the people with the skills set, and also the people with the EQ [emotional quotient, or intelligence] to be able to manage the change within the organization."*

Of course, CMOs need to bring on new marketing talent to address the gaps in their current capabilities, but it is also important to think one step ahead. Try to anticipate new needs before they become urgent, and look for people who can contribute to the overall organizational goals rather than just fill an immediate functional need in the marketing team. *"For us, looking for talent and bringing in subject matter experts who can help us boost our efforts to be a next-generation bank—that's really important as it relates to our hiring model,"* says Jennifer Breithaupt of Citi. *"We have to always be looking across the whole team, all the teams and thinking, 'What don't we have? What are we not anticipating? Where can we find the talent that can help us stay ahead of that?'"*

Syl Saller of Diageo also drives home the point that she not only looks for a balance of skills, but maintains high expectations of everyone. *"I'm always looking at the constellation of the team to ensure we have the right mix of skills. Leadership is expected from everyone at every level,"* says Saller. *"It doesn't matter if you don't have people reporting to you—everyone is leading something: a project, agencies, cross functional teams."*

> *"I'm always looking at the constellation of the team to ensure we have the right mix of skills. Leadership is expected from everyone at every level. It doesn't matter if you don't have people reporting to you—everyone is leading something: a project, agencies, cross functional teams."*
>
> **SYL SALLER**
> Diageo

CORPORATE LEARNING FOR THE DIGITAL AGE

In the 1960s, companies like GE and McDonald's revolutionized the work environment by providing internal training for their employees, enabling them to learn new (mostly manual) skills and to further develop their careers. In the late 1990s and 2000s, companies like Apple, Boeing, and Danone again paved the way for more of a modern training mindset that sought to develop executive and leadership capabilities. Today, corporate learning must involve bolstering skills beyond management and leadership. It needs to facilitate knowledge about new digital tools and platforms, as well as encourage knowledge sharing and employee interactions across departments. *"Most people are so excited to learn. They want to be re-skilled, and I think that's part of it. How do we take this as an opportunity to re-skill a lot of our folks on what they have and build off of it?"* asks Meredith Verdone of Bank of America. *"It's not so much about bringing in all these people to different skill sets, but about how we give people a growth opportunity to be successful."*

CASE STUDY

 **#BEMORE**

1 **BACKGROUND:** Citi is a 200-year-old financial institution with an established history. To be able to survive for such a long time, companies need to be adaptable and innovative. In order to drive change within their organization, Citi ran a 30-day challenge for their staff to #BeMore by learning continuously. The campaign encouraged earning through a series of small actions embedded into their everyday workflow—leading to several awards for the team. The campaign was built around three global objectives: building leadership and manager capability, driving ethical and cultural change, and empowering employee-led development. One of its unique features is the use of social learning to educate people about what and how they learn, while simultaneously providing a central access point for all things learning across the region.

2 **PROCESS:** In late 2015, the EMEA L&D team at Citi launched the #BeMore campaign. This internal program was designed to empower employees to take control of their own development and facilitate behavioral change across Citi's organization. They sought to introduce continuous workplace learning based on the principles of 70:20:10 and known at Citi as the 3E's: Experience, Exposure, Education. A year from its inception, more staff have completed their individual development plans, with #BeMore activities being embedded into the everyday actions of the business. The challenges comprised of 30 micro actions that were designed to challenge individuals to do everyday activities differently, building muscle memory and beginning to form new habits. Each micro action took less than ten minutes to complete.

3 **RESULTS:** In the first six months after the program's launch, more than 12,000 participated in the program via the Jive-based social platform, Citi Collaborate. Participants were asked to share their learning with their colleagues via Citi Collaborate, and more than 4,500 people uploaded comments and photos, liking and sharing their colleagues' contributions. Citi has seen a steady improvement in the levels of engagement over the program's lifetime, and more importantly, they've seen a shift away from reliance on traditional training with a push toward ongoing learning—supported by tools and technology that are learner-led that will continue to develop as the program matures.

This applies to everyone in the company, from the entry-level all the way to senior leadership. *"What we see here is a rapid evolution of digital across the business where we're expecting all of our demand leaders, as well as local market marketing directors, really to be increasingly tech and digitally savvy,"* says Andrew Clarke of Mars.

Colgate-Palmolive also created a training program for senior leadership which they call Building Brands at Colgate. *"We held a global brand summit of 100 marketing leaders from around the world. We got all of them together for a one-week program and we spent a day and a half on digital transformation,"* says Mukul Deoras of Colgate-Palmolive. *"We took the seemingly complex topic of impactful brand engagement and made it very simple, bite sized. Every single marketing director in the Colgate world came here and got exposed and trained. This kind of training is key to the re-skilling of the organization."*

While it may be tempting to fill digital gaps exclusively with outside hires, training existing staff in digital capabilities has a significant advantage. Namely, they are already well-versed in the company's history, culture, processes, and brand identity—which can sometimes be more of an advantage than having a niche digital skill. *"We have taken lessons from design thinking and held workshops around the world to up-skill our colleagues,"* says Maryam Banikarim of Hyatt Hotels. *"We're doing the same with training around digital skill sets. To succeed you have to invest in continued professional development because the technology moves at an unprecedented pace, and because your people are your most valuable asset."*

Building capabilities for existing talent has many benefits. For employees, it creates a more dynamic environment, which sets up a road for growth and forward movement. For companies, especially in the departments that require an understanding of digital capabilities and technology like marketing and IT, digital upskilling creates talent who are cross functional; they are able to approach a problem from several different angles. Creating your own supply of digitally savvy employees also helps you build the people you want from the ground up, as opposed to always looking outside the organization for people to fill gaps. *"One of my biggest goals is to build the most powerful marketing team with capability of running a global marketing campaign both on a digital and offline basis,"* says YH Lee of Samsung. *"In addition to our existing marketing competencies, we emphasize and provide support for continuous learning across a wide range of digital technologies as well as the ability to read and analyze data."*

This can also work in the opposite direction, where marketers with strong digital backgrounds are trained to have a strong grasp of traditional marketing. *"It's difficult because it's new. Everybody is moving in that direction, and there is limited supply. More and more we're going to have to build the capability internally,"* says David Timm of Pizza Hut. *"Then there is also the challenge that when you hire performance marketing people, they have a lot to learn about our business and traditional marketing. I think the nature of mass marketing is going to change a lot in the next few years, but it's still going to be a very important part of our business."* In essence, training helps build a truly modern marketing professional. *"In general, we have to be teaching our performance marketers how to do the more traditional marketing and vice versa. The attraction for anyone who joins us is that they can become complete marketers. Ultimately this conversation goes away and it's just marketing that is inclusive of the old and the new. We're a few years away from that,"* Timm adds.

Raja Rajamannar of Mastercard echoes this sentiment:

When you look at talent, you've got classical marketers and you've got contemporary marketers. The classical marketers are from the packaged goods type, like me, who have been trained about consumer psychology, positioning brands, and all those good things. These folks are less comfortable, if not less proficient, on digital, data, tech, experimentation, and testing. On the other hand, if you look at the contemporary marketers, they are good at all of these things, but not good at the fundamentals of marketing, the first principles… To get both of these people, it's next to impossible. What we started doing is doing an intense amount of cross-training between the two, and we now have around 20 to 25 certification programs internally that were created specifically for cross-training.

DIGITAL TRAINING AT SCALE

A curriculum for the digital age requires new platforms so that it can be spread across markets for global companies. Creating an advanced digital learning experience platform not only allows trainings to be deployed across nations and around the world, but they also serve well to track and store learning records for accurate learning analytics—and to track how different markets and sections are doing in their training journey.

Colgate-Palmolive partnered with a digital learning agency called General Assembly, who created a learning curriculum for them. Mukul Deoras and his team then shared this with 500 people around the world who had to complete at least ten courses in a year (although they could do up to 30 courses, depending on their interest levels). *"It was like a customized journey for each person that started with an assessment of their basic knowledge of digital and then created a personalized curriculum. This had a tremendous organic response. We did not force it on people,"* says Deoras. *"Marketing professionals today are hungry to increase their knowledge of these new ways of building brands in a digital first era. Strong leadership is important in this journey. All of us have to constantly talk about digital transformation again, and again, and again. We have to make sure that people hear the senior leadership talking about transformation."*

FIGURE 42

LEARNING
AT THE SPEED OF BUSINESS

Physical separation from the "daily grind" to develop new skills and behavior

Cloud-based learning that is mobile and multiplatform

Mobile platforms for learning at your fingertips

In-person classroom experiences that are high impact and immersive

THE CORPORATE ACADEMY OF THE FUTURE

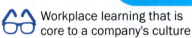

Workplace learning that is core to a company's culture

Analytics for learning to enhance performance and measure impact

A culture of social learning, real-time feedback, sharing, and networking

Use of big data and predictive analytics to improve learning continually

LEARN FROM THE OUTSIDE

Even if it's outside the realm of formal training, Raja Rajamannar of Mastercard drives home the point that CMOs should still go out of their way to understand what others are doing. This seems like such a small, straightforward task, and yet is often overlooked or brushed aside.

"I'll just do a simple thing. Somebody comes and says, 'Artificial intelligence in marketing.' I'll ask them, 'What is it that you can do or what is it that you do. Let me understand that.' If it is something which makes sense, I'll say okay, let's do a pilot. I cannot afford to build internal talent everywhere. So, the external sources are educating me quite a lot and I really take it seriously," says Rajamannar.

Shell also employs this strategy when it comes to training. They often send employees to outside organizations to pick up new skills, and apply those learnings internally when the employee returns. *"The basic information of what has changed in marketing, what have we learned, where is our work most effective—that's available to all marketers,"* says Linda van Schaik of Shell. *"We use a blended training program, online apps with bite-sized updates, but we also have in-person programs as well. We also have people work in start-ups or digital ventures, and then take them back so that they bring in that learning as well."*

REVERSE MENTORSHIP & LEADERSHIP TRAINING

Perhaps one of the most interesting dynamics of this digital age is that the leadership of an organization often has just as much to learn as middle-management, or sometimes even entry-level hires. This creates a unique environment in which cross-training can reach across traditional company hierarchies. Raja Rajamannar of Mastercard uses reverse mentoring as an important educational tool. *"I get reverse mentoring and it does three things. Number one, it helps me stay abreast of trends. Second, I get to know my talent deeply. Third, I hope I add value to them through these interactions."* Employing reverse mentorship programs where younger, more digitally fluent talent trains leadership on new technology and trends can be cost effective, empowering, and sustainable.

Leveraging reverse mentoring is a great way to use internal resources. Training doesn't always have to come from external partners, and holding these types of internal digital trainings for the senior leadership can help them stay engaged with their team, while simultaneously plunging them headfirst into the world of a "digital native."

"I try to keep myself up to date because the rate of obsolescence is so fast," Rajamannar says. *"If you don't stay on top, you're obsolete."*

THE EIGHT ACTIONS OF A FUTURE FIT CMO

Digital transformation is an ever-evolving process. As new technologies enter the market and disruptors continue to spring up and challenge entire categories to think fast and react more nimbly, traditional marketing organizations will have to always be thinking two steps ahead. The rapid integration of digital into nearly every aspect of marketing has completely changed the way marketers interact with both their consumers and other branches inside their own companies. As evident from the CMOs featured in this book, it's oftentimes up to the marketing function to lead the larger organizational transformation. Throughout the course of writing this book, we highlighted common themes running through each conversation. As a result, we identified Eight Actions of a Future Fit CMO. Of course, no one can predict exactly what the future holds. However, these eight action items are the best ways that Chief Marketing Officers can work to meet the digital transformation wave head-on.

1. NEVER STOP LEARNING

Continuous education is incredibly important in an environment where the pace of change is certain to move along at a constant, speedy clip. CMOs need to stay up-to-date on all things digital, from the newest platforms and channels, to the latest technology solutions. The most successful CMOs know that whatever formula worked in the past likely won't continue to work in the future. There has to be steady, forward-thinking change. *"Having a clear vision and strategy—and not being everywhere [and] trying to be everything for everyone—and challenging ourselves every day on how can we be faster, smarter, [and] better is something we have to remind ourselves about every day,"* says Jennifer Breithaupt of Citi. *"We cannot do what we used to do. It's not lather, rinse, and repeat. It's about what's next, and what does that look like, and being open to it."*

Since no CMO can be an expert on every topic, the education of all senior marketing leadership is a crucial component to success. This education can come in many forms, whether it's digital training sessions or frequent face-to-face meetings of global leadership to make sure everyone stays current on the realities of each market. David Roman of Lenovo emphasizes the importance of understanding the business climates of different countries:

One thing that makes Lenovo different is that it truly is a global company. I've always worked for what I thought were global companies, like Apple and HP. These are global companies geographically, but they really are American companies that have grown outside of the US. Lenovo, just because of the way we came about, we're really a global company. We have a leadership team with fifteen people. We basically meet once a month, a different country every month. We just rotate around the world. We get to experience all of the different countries just by physically being there, and that's great.

Ensuring that each team member is set up for success needs to be a priority for a CMO at the forefront of this digital transformation journey. *"One of my personal goals is to drive capability transformation. I prioritize that above everything else,"* says Mukul Deoras of Colgate-Palmolive. *"There are senior leaders in my team who are responsible for category and brand strategies. I do what others will not have time to do, which is to build capabilities."*

Of all the traits of a successful CMO, curiosity and the desire to learn are two of the most important. *"I've always been curious. Frankly, I am excited about what I don't know,"* says David Timm of Pizza Hut. He continues:

I would say seven, eight months ago, I was quintessentially a traditional marketer. Digital transformation is the reason that I'm excited because I feel that, after many years of being an expert in traditional marketing, there's this new complementary space. It's great to be learning so much at this stage in my career. Before I started this journey, I spent time with Google, Facebook, and CMOs who are operating in e-commerce environments. [I got involved in] academics, and reading books, and just trying to understand this world so that I could lead in a space that's not where my experience lies. What motivates me is that I can see there's a real opportunity here, and I feel as though I'm growing in the process.

2. FIGHT FOR TALENT

A recent report from the ANA titled "Bridging the Talent Disconnect: Charting the Pathways to Future Growth,"[1] asserts that college graduates are turning away from careers in marketing, leading both the client and agency sides to experience a "talent crunch." The study cites "a looming marketing and advertising talent crisis" driven in part by a lack of common vision, language, and perceived relevance among marketers, young professionals, and the colleges and universities where they graduate. The ANA identified four key drivers of this so-called talent crisis.

FIGURE 43

FOUR KEY DRIVERS OF
THE MARKETING TALENT CRUNCH:

1 Digital transformation is complicating new marketing and advertising career paths

2 Clients and agencies are now directly competing with technology companies for highly skilled talent

3 The expectations of today's young talent differs from previous generations

4 University curricula cannot keep up with the rapid change going on in the industry

In order to prepare for the looming storm, investing in finding the right talent while also educating existing talent within an organization should be a top priority for a Future Fit CMO. *"In the end, it's all about your people. You can have a great strategy, but you need people who are willing to take the hill,"* says Maryam Banikarim of Hyatt Hotels. David Timm of Pizza Hut echoes her sentiment, highlighting that external partners also need to be included in the process of talent education:

I would say that we're early on the journey, and we're probably late getting started. We are dealing with it in a number of different ways. Firstly, it's around capabilities. We need to be building the capability internally. We're attacking that through a combination of recruitment as well as putting together programs to educate our existing marketing team. There's also a component of 'just do it'—get out there and try and test and learn. A big piece of digital performance marketing is to educate our existing system, including our partners on the need for change.

At the end of the day, marketing is an industry built around people and relationships. For a CMO, finding the right talent starts by getting familiar with the talent pool available on the market. *"I get motivated by people, by meeting people who are in similar and sometimes vastly different ends of this business,"* says Linda Boff of GE. *"But I color this business very broadly so I love meeting with people from all different industries and business types—people in the start-up community, art, and design. Everyone."*

A recent study on the marketing hiring landscape from McKinley Marketing Partners[2] revealed that now is the best time to be a digital marketer looking for work. Figures for 2017 showed that 56 percent of the positions that were open among the 300 survey respondents were for digital-specific positions, while only 24 percent of marketers were actively looking for work in that sector. The only discipline where supply significantly outpaced demand was "traditional marketing," indicating that traditional marketers looking for work might face a certain level of difficulty.

3. BECOME CUSTOMER ADVOCATES

One of the biggest themes running throughout this book is that the consumer is now in the front seat driving marketing trends. The level of engagement between consumers and brands is the highest it has ever been. It is crucial for marketers to have an open dialogue with their target audience, to understand and respond to their needs. *"I have this saying, 'In marketing, we are the voice of and the voice to the customer,'"* says Meredith Verdone of Bank of America. She continues:

By the voice of, I mean we understand them, we're the advocate for them, and we know their needs and wants. Once we have this, we become the voice to, meaning that we create and develop all communications and the strategies, and deliver it to them. If you're the voice of and the voice to, you're certainly going to be welcome at the table to influence all the customer experience.... Where marketing begins and ends, it's really very gray right now. What we're really focused on is understanding that fully integrated experience, because that's how customers see the world. Whether they experience us through the app where we have 24 million active mobile users, from an email, or by actually visiting a financial center. To them, it's all one brand.

Consumer expectation about how brands will interact with them has dramatically changed in the past decade. Before, mass marketing was the norm, and consumers expected to see ads that weren't necessarily relevant to their lives or needs. Now, according to Salesforce's recent report called "The State of the Connected Consumer,"[3] people expect to be treated like an individual, rather than a number. Of the 7,000 surveyed consumers, 72 percent of consumers and 89 percent of business buyers say that they expect companies to understand their unique expectations and needs, while 66 percent of consumers say they're likely to switch brands if they feel treated like a number, not an individual. A consumer-centric strategy has become indispensable with driving loyalty. The other major factor influencing brand loyalty is consistency across channels. According to Salesforce, 75 percent of consumers expect consistent experiences across multiple channels (in-person, social, web, mobile), with 73 percent more likely to switch brands if they don't get this. *"Obviously, digital transformation has changed customer behavior and their expectations of us in terms of where and how they want brands to communicate and interact with them,"* says Jennifer Breithaupt of Citi. *"It's forced us as a brand to rapidly evolve from a traditional standard marketing mix model to implementing a holistic, omni-channel, connected approach to all of our marketing."*

FIGURE 44

2017 DEMAND FOR SKILLS WITHIN CREATIVE SERVICES

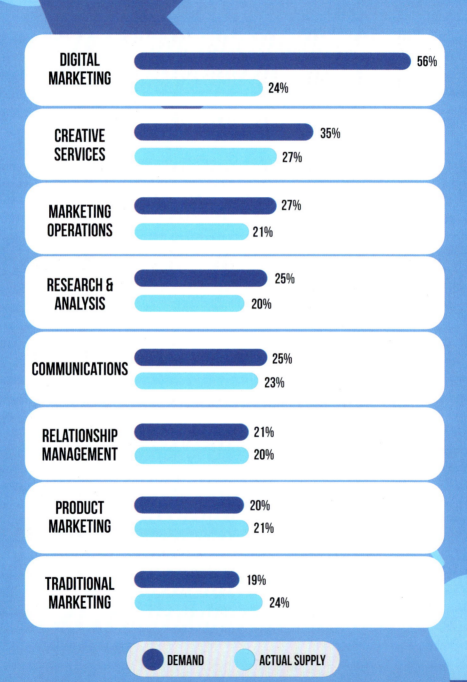

DIGITAL MARKETING
56%
24%

CREATIVE SERVICES
35%
27%

MARKETING OPERATIONS
27%
21%

RESEARCH & ANALYSIS
25%
20%

COMMUNICATIONS
25%
23%

RELATIONSHIP MANAGEMENT
21%
20%

PRODUCT MARKETING
20%
21%

TRADITIONAL MARKETING
19%
24%

DEMAND   ACTUAL SUPPLY

4. ADOPT A BUSINESS MINDSET

In order for marketing to return to the boardroom around the globe, the best CMOs have invested time to truly understand the fundamentals of their company's business, not just how their work impacts awareness, consideration, and purchase intent. In R3's consulting work, our most successful client marketers will often be a critical part of investor relations meetings, annual shareholder events, and sales conferences. It's all about the mindset and the desire to make a tangible difference.

This carries over to the process of deciding how to approach digital transformation. C-suite executives often have to make tough decisions about how and where to invest their budget to adopt new tools and processes. The answer is, of course, different for each organization. But one thing is clear: technology for technology's sake never works. Each brand has to decide how to make digital work for them, using it to highlight the strengths that already exist in the brand DNA and enhance its business function. *"We're making very specific investments in technology. Yet, what is special and unique about us?"* asks Peter Nowlan of Four Seasons Hotels and Resorts. *"It's our personal, direct connection. We know that most people will go online to access information, but in the end they still want to talk to a real person at Four Seasons before booking."*

GE is perhaps the best example of adopting a comprehensive digital transformation strategy while staying true to their business in the process. *"We're a big company,"* says Linda Boff of GE. *"We're in over 180 countries; we have hundreds of thousands of employees. Big companies can show up in a way that is very faceless, very corporate, and unapproachable. We've tried to do exactly the opposite. We've tried to be human, we've tried to be at times humorous and whimsical, but always, always a human, authentic approach. The more human, the better."*

Many organizations have used acquisition as a technique to bolster their digital offerings, but this can be a tough space to navigate. CMOs need to ask themselves how well the company they're acquiring fits in with the DNA of the larger organization, and whether it is an offering that their consumers want and need, to ensure that the acquisition is being made for the right reasons. *"In pet care, we invested heavily in acquiring businesses in the vet services space to complement our businesses in pet nutrition,"* says Andrew Clarke of Mars. He continues:

Really, investing for the future from a business model perspective, that's the sort of business which gives us data, expertise, and scale into new areas which I think enables us to innovate in new and different ways. For example, we bought a small business called Whistle relatively recently. It acts like a Fitbit for dogs to really measure their movement and diet. Also, that then helps to have a better data set to innovate in the pet space.

Some global marketers have already made significant headway on their digital transformation journeys, but one of the main reasons for this success is the realization that it is, in fact, a journey. Once you become complacent in this new world of marketing, you get left behind. *"We are on a transformational journey,"* says Raja Rajamannar of Mastercard. *"I feel very gratified that our Board of Directors has told us that the difference between how the marketing function is working at Mastercard today compared to in the past is night and day."*

5. FORM A NEW APPROACH TO PARTNERS

For a CMO, knowing when to go outside of the organization to find the right external talent is equally as important as investing in internal talent. *"We define partners very broadly—creative agencies, media partners, tech partners, entrepreneurs, and design partners. The list goes on and on,"* says Syl Saller of Diageo. *"We have a disciplined way of managing our creative roster in which the senior marketing leadership team evaluates our work annually and provides feedback to our agencies."* Finding the right partners can be challenging, but taking a new and innovative approach to agency search can make all the difference. At Diageo, Saller and her team have developed a plan for partners they want to trial. She explains:

In looking for entrepreneurial or tech partners, we evaluate over 3,000 companies a year through our distill and tech venture arms of our futures team. This also provides us with a clear idea of what the latest trends are, and who is doing the best work. For example, we can see that everyone is moving into the home delivery space and we choose to partner with those who best meet customer needs and where we can create a win-win relationship.

Managing partnerships is its own art form; it takes patience and a willingness to work hard and communicate often. The challenges associated with external partners will only continue to grow, as Future Fit CMOs will also have to manage a roster including both traditional agencies and technology vendors going forward. Forming these new partnerships is an important strategy for David Timm of Pizza Hut, who says:

There's an African proverb that says, 'You learn to cut down trees by cutting down trees.' We're encouraging people to take risks, to experiment, and to partner with the big tech companies—Google and Facebook, et cetera—to just go and test what's possible. As we get learnings from one market, we transfer them to other markets. It's going to give us momentum and give us the evidence of return on investment. That creates a repeatable model and the rest becomes self-fulfilling.

Aligning agency partners to drive mutual success starts with the CMO. Relationships that don't align on mutual goals tend to fall apart relatively quickly, and marketing goals can change based on an organization's wider business targets. *"We need agency partners that completely understand that, at the end of the day, we have to bring more guests into our restaurants,"* says Axel Schwan of Burger King. He continues:

We have to drive traffic and we have to drive sales because the best measure of brand health is an ever-increasing number of guests. We have elements in our branch tracker that allow us to measure brand health directly, all around the world, so we can drive traffic and sales using the brand-specific attributes we identify. Once an agency partner understands those goals, and the drivers we're using to achieve them, we can become one united team and have a great relationship. Good communication helps us achieve that.

Beyond agencies, the best CMOs are now leveraging the entire ecosystem in their favor—with regular visits to Mountain View, Menlo Park, and Seattle, as well as Shenzhen and Hangzhou. They are active participants with key media and asset managers, and they're using their procurement teams as value creators not cost reducers. In short, they are gaining leverage—from their competitors and from the traditional approach.

6. MEASURE IT TO MOVE IT

Marketers today have the tools to show how their work impacts sales. In order for CMOs to strengthen their position in the boardroom, it is critical that they do this. *"Going forward, everything we do is a link into the top of the house,"* says Meredith Verdone of Bank of America. *"It's not like marketing is off doing their own thing over in the corner. Everything is aligned to the company and our company is driving responsible growth, which means growing in a sustainable way, in a customer-centric way."*

One key component of linking marketing activities to business goals at large is breaking down organizational silos to foster cross-team collaboration. Mukul Deoras of Colgate-Palmolive highlights the importance of sales and marketing departments working together going forward:

Increasingly, a significant chunk of the impressions that we create through digital media, whether they are banners or videos, are actually created from customer partner websites like walmart.com or chewy.com or petsmart.com. Take Alibaba, it's a classic example. A reasonable amount of consumer engagement actually happens on Alibaba's website. Now, who should manage that relationship? If that relationship is managed by sales, and the marketing people are not involved, we may lose focus on brand building and consistency. If it is only marketing and the salespeople are not involved, it also won't be ideal as the razor-sharp focus on transaction would be missing. I think the boundaries have blurred so much because media engagement and transactions have merged into one, we have no option but to come together as marketing and sales and work together.

Many CMOs have already taken great strides to prove the ROI of their marketing activities. Examples include the Priceless Engine at Mastercard and Catalyst at Diageo, both analytics tools allowing for real-time ROI analysis. For today's CMOs, becoming Future Fit will be about tying all of their activities to the organization's business objectives. Not just campaigns, but each aspect of the marketing function. Everything, from how talent is hired to how partnerships are managed, can circle back to driving business goals. *"You need to listen hard, but you have to have your own North Star about what's right, or you'll get whipped around by everyone's perspectives,"* says Syl Saller of Diageo. *"And if that North Star is truly rooted in growth of the business—rather than ego, or what your team wants—your chances of success are much higher."*

7. RUN FAST AND BREAK (SOME) THINGS

With due deference to Mr. Zuckerberg, the best companies are using a portion of their marketing budgets to test and learn at scale. Large marketing organizations have large talent pools and marketing budgets on their side, and should dedicate a certain portion of these resources to staying ahead of digital trends, rather than waiting until they're in the midst of disruption to tackle issues. Taking calculated risks can help CMOs stay ahead of disruption and stay relevant to their consumers. *"Doing stuff that's more innovative, and perhaps a little bit more risky, using data and technology in new and different ways, they're very much helping to grow our existing brands and keeping it relevant in today's world,"* says Andrew Clarke of Mars.

Staying ahead of disruption requires CMOs to not only know where their competitors are in the digital transformation journey, but they also need to be attuned to where their customers are. *"The DNA of GE, at its very core, is invention, going back to Edison 125 years ago,"* says Linda Boff of GE. She continues:

Find out what the world needs, and then proceed to invent it. I think the best brands, in my opinion, have intense self-awareness. We really understand this, and I like to believe that we are one of them. We really understand who we are and what we are not and where that gives us permission to play quite authentically. And for us, it has been science, technology, innovation which has led us to be on tech platforms because that's where we're going to reach audiences that are like-minded. It's where we're going to reach early adopters.

Leveraging technology in new and interesting ways is going to allow CMOs to help their brands rise above the noise. The challenge will be finding a balance between being present across new touchpoints in the consumer journey and being too invasive in consumers' lives. The rise of the IoT means that consumers are wearing digital devices, like Apple Watches and Fitbits, and have connected devices all throughout their homes, such as smart appliances and Amazon Echoes. New campaigns that feature these types of technologies are already sparking a debate in the advertising industry about how far is too far when it comes to marketing in this new digital age.

CASE STUDY

 HOME OF THE WHOPPER

1 **BACKGROUND:** Burger King traditionally advertises with 15 second TV spots, but wanted to come up with a creative way to extend that time to talk about their signature burger, The Whopper, without buying a 30 second spot. To deliver their full message, the TV spot intentionally triggered Google Home to read the Wikipedia entry for The Whopper by including the phrase, "Ok Google, what is the Whopper Burger?" The result was that Burger King essentially hacked the Google Home device with its ad, turning a 15 second spot into a viral marketing stunt.

2 **PROCESS:** After the spot was launched online, the Google Home devices were initially answering the question as planned. However, it wasn't long before people started changing The Whopper's Wikipedia page to include some pretty bad ingredients. After the Wikipedia page was restored, Google decided to block their devices from responding to the phrase. Burger King's solution was to edit the audio on the TV spot, effectively getting around Google's block and activating the devices again. Eventually, Google gave up on trying to block the phrase from activating the devices, and a debate ensued about the limits of advertising and the intrusiveness of smart home devices, while successfully putting The Whopper at the top of millions of people's minds.

3 **RESULTS:** The stunt was incredibly successful, garnering $35 million in earned media and becoming a global trending topic across several platforms. The spot saw 15 million organic online views in the first 48 hours alone, and the burger shop saw a 500% increase in brand mentions online. The spot quickly became the most talked about TV spot in Burger King's history. The stunt propelled David Miami to win the Grand Prix in Direct Marketing at Cannes in 2017, prevailing over the year's most popular ad, Fearless Girl, by just one vote. The spot was called "the best abuse of technology" by one of the jurors.

While using technology in an authentic way to reach digitally savvy consumers is the right mindset to adopt, the speed of change is definitely a challenge for large legacy organizations. *"Everything is moving faster. The speed of products to market, the speed of competitors following, the speed of brands gaining and losing relevance,"* says Andres Kiger of Converse. He continues:

In the past, every company could afford to just do one or two things, and then just let it sit there and let it simmer for a while. For a brand today to be connected, it will need to learn how to become an authentic part of a conversation, knowing when to join and also when to step away. This new approach to brand building means that basic foundations, including team skills, structure, partners, and levels of investments, need to be revisited. It is certainly an exciting time for marketing visionaries to design a new future. Fun times ahead, but certainly not for the faint-hearted.

8. REMAIN A STORYTELLER

No matter what lies ahead in the future of digital, the one thing a truly Future Fit CMO can't forget is that storytelling still lies at the heart of marketing. The tools to relay these stories will always change and evolve, but brands that dilute their DNA with an overdependence on data will lose what most consumers love about them. Bank of America's Meredith Verdone points out the importance of keeping long-term goals in mind, rather than getting lost in short-term results:

We have a couple of different levels of messaging that we do. One is what we call demand gen, which is really a lower funnel kind of activity. How do we generate business? We've got the upper funnel, which is how do we tell our story. As a CMO, I want to make sure that we're telling our story too. We're always about long-term growth and sustainable growth and not just the short term profitability.

This rings true across all industries. *"We have to be clear in storytelling. Understanding what the conflict is, what the monster is. We're a human- and people-oriented brand and our monster is people skimming through life, being ruled by the algorithm, the impersonal nature of information overload,"* says Peter Nowlan of Four Seasons Hotels and Resorts. *"Our challenge is to continue to nurture the human connection when faced with this conflict. People may have thousands of friends on social media, but they may not actually know the names of their neighbors. They are looking for those real connections and Four Seasons is in a unique position to provide them."*

Moving forward, CMOs and marketers need to explore a balance of digital options that help advance the company narrative. Linda Boff of GE sums it up the best, saying, *"Whether it's a way to tell a story, a platform to tell a story, or a way to sell that is different, [we have to ask] how can we use digital tools? How can we find markets and penetrate them with the best of what digital enables us to do?"*

WHAT LIES AHEAD?

The future of marketing is full of possibilities. For 100 years, brands marketed *to* people. With the growth of social and digital, they started to market *with* people. In the future, brands will be expected to market *for* people and provide a real utility that makes their lives easier. Many CMOs are already taking steps to make sure their messages align with new consumer trends, as evident by the growing popularity of corporate social responsibility and brands' increasing tendency to take social and political stances that align with their consumers' core values.

For many CMOs, the biggest challenge lies in what they don't know. Jennifer Breithaupt of Citi asserts, *"The landscape is moving and changing and evolving so quickly, the biggest challenge is what don't we know? What's the next new thing?"* The combination of the unknown with the rapid speed of change can be daunting for a CMO, but with the right mix of tools and talent, there is more opportunity than ever to form deeper relationships with consumers and truly effect change within an organization. *"The marketing function is now seen as a business driver and a significant partner in winning new business and keeping existing business,"* says Raja Rajamannar of Mastercard. *"My vision is, and we are not there yet, but my vision is that when asked, 'What is the biggest competitive advantage for Mastercard?' I want the answer to be marketing."*

There's endless opportunity through technology and data to know more. *"I've heard, 'The pace of change today will be the slowest you'll ever experience.' It'll never be as slow as it is right now. Today is the 'good old days,'"* says Linda Boff of GE. She continues:

CASE STUDY

Colgate® **#EVERYDROPCOUNTS**

1 **BACKGROUND:** With one in ten people worldwide with no access to clean water, raising awareness of the importance of conservation is incredibly important. To help shed light on global water shortages, Colgate-Palmolive created the #EveryDrop-Counts campaign with a video communication illustrating how a seemingly small act, like turning off the faucet while brushing your teeth, can make a big difference. Since then, this message has been shared in over 70 countries around the world, including via an ad during Super Bowl 50 in the US, and has had significant traction on social media, where it has been viewed millions of times. To adapt the campaign and appeal to a broad base, Colgate and Michael Phelps partnered up to help remind people to save water.

2 **PROCESS:** Colgate wanted to make an impassioned plea from the King of Water himself. After the partnership was announced, the CGP giant leveraged several channels to get the message out. They used videos on Snapchat, as well as a Facebook Live Q&A with Phelps, to talk about how to save water. They also partnered with Vice media to make short films showing what it would be like if you left other things running, like coffee and gasoline, as well as to make a documentary featuring Phelps. Vice hosted an online custom content hub featuring water saving techniques. Finally, they launched a TV spot that featured both Phelps and his son.

3 **RESULTS:** The launch of the Save Water Campaign featuring Michael Phelps was a success, and has garnered over 1 billion impressions online. Colgate has made water a global sustainability priority, recognizing the responsibility that businesses have in addressing the global issue of water security. Colgate's broader global "Save Water" initiative started as part of the company's long-standing commitment to promoting water conservation awareness to all of its global consumers by 2020. Colgate works consistently to reduce their water-use footprint, having avoided enough water consumption in manufacturing to fill nearly 20,000 competition-sized swimming pools since 2002. However, 90 percent of Colgate's current water-use footprint comes from consumer use of their products so they are constantly innovating new ways to ask consumers for their help.

So, if today is the good old days and we have at our fingertips the tools to know more about our customers and our markets, the onus I think is on CMOs to know what's knowable, then to take that information and translate it into the right insights that allow us to tell and to sell. I'm an optimist, so I will always be a little bullish, but I'm quite bullish on the role of the CMO who embraces all that we are now able to embrace.

The type of agility necessary to tackle the changing landscape head on will need support from other functions in the organization. Mukul Deoras of Colgate-Palmolive points this out:

Technically, the CIO has knowledge about this new territory, but no experience. The Chief Sales Officer has an understanding of the customer, but has no experience in consumer engagement. Marketing people have tools at their disposal, whether it's media or promotion, but now need to constantly keep changing the tools, drive demand, and make changes happen. This kind of agility is a big challenge that we face. Marketing agility is going to be in big demand. For agility, you require help—you cannot do this on your own.

CMOs have the resources behind them to take the lead on digital transformation, but to be truly Future Fit, they will have to do their best to figure out "the next big thing." It is common in the industry to hear that there is no such thing as digital marketing anymore—it's just marketing. If that is the case, what is the next stage of marketing transformation? Maryam Banikarim of Hyatt Hotels sums it up perfectly: *"Today, it's about digital. Who knows what tomorrow's going to be about? We're all going to be responsible for figuring that out."*

REFERENCES: ENDNOTES

CHAPTER 1

1. Mangles, Carolanne. "State of digital marketing 2017." Smart Insights, last modified September 14, 2017.https://www.smartinsights.com/managing-digital-marketing/marketing-innovation/state-of-digital-marketing/attachment/state-of-digital-marketing-2017/.

2. "Cisco Visual Networking Index: Forecast and Methodology, 2016–2021." Cisco Systems, last modified September 15, 2017. https://www.cisco.com/c/en/us/solutions/collateral/service-provider/visual-networking-index-vni/complete-white-paper-c11-481360.html

3. Mangles, Carolanne. "State of digital marketing 2017." Smart Insights, Technology for Marketing. last modified September 14, 2017.https://www.smartinsights.com/managing-digital-marketing/marketing-innovation/state-of-digital-marketing/attachment/state-of-digital-marketing-2017/.

4. "Executives Championing Digital Transformation Efforts." Altimeter Group, 2014. http://www.platformc2e.nl/wp022014/wp-content/uploads/Figure-5.jpg

5. Solis, Brian. "What's Driving Digital Transformation Across Organizations?" September 16, 2016. http://www2.prophet.com/The-2016-State-of-Digital-Transformation

CHAPTER 2

1. Christensen, Clayton M., Raynor, Michael E., McDonald, Rory. "What is Disruptive Innovation?" Harvard Business Review. https://hbr.org/2015/12/what-is-disruptive-innovation

2. "Dell Technologies Research: 78% of Businesses Feel Threatened by Digital Start-ups" Dell Technologies. https://www.delltechnologies.com/en-us/press/unveiling-the-digital-transformation-index.htm

3. Tolon, Zeynep. "How CMOs should prepare for digital disruption." IBM. Last modified December 2, 2015. https://www.ibm.com/blogs/insights-on-business/gbs-strategy/how-cmos-should-prepare-for-digital-disruption/

4. Boncheck, Mark, Cornfield, Gene. "There Are 4 Futures for CMOs (Some Better Than Others)" Harvard Business Review. September 18, 2017. https://hbr.org/2017/09/there-are-4-futures-for-cmos-some-better-than-others

5. "2017 Predictions: Dynamics That Will Shape The Future In The Age Of The Customer." Forrester, October 2016. https://go.forrester.com/wp-content/uploads/Forrester-2017-Predictions.pdf

6. Quiring, Kevin; Barton, Rachel E.; Levesque, Joanna. "The C-level disruptive growth opportunity." Accenture Strategy, 2016. https://www.accenture.com/

t20170124T041545Z__w__/us-en/_acn-media/PDF-33/Accenture-CMO-IN-SIGHTS-POV-FINAL.pdf#zoom=50

7. "The Next Wave Of Digital Marketing Is Predictive." Forrester Consulting, Rocket Fuel. August, 2017. https://rocketfuel.com/wp-content/uploads/Forrester-TLP-The-Next-Wave-Of-Digital-Marketing-Is-Predic-tive-August-2017.pdf

CHAPTER 3

1. McNair, Corey. "Worldwide Retail and Ecommerce Sales: eMarketer's Estimates for 2016–2021." eMarketer. July 18, 2017. https://www.emarketer.com/Report/Worldwide-Re-tail-Ecommerce-Sales-eMarketers-Esti-mates-20162021/2002090

2. Satchu, Jamil; Chang, Connie. "Winning the CPG Zero-Sum Game by Uncovering Hidden Growth Pockets." IRI. February, 2017. https://www.iriworldwide.com/IRI/media/2017-Demand-Portfolio.pdf

3. Keshia Hannam. "A Record Amount of Brick and Mortar Stores Will Close in 2017" Fortune Magazine. October 26, 2017. http://fortune.com/2017/10/26/a-record-amount-of-brick-and-mortar-stores-will-close-in-2017/

4. "The Store of the Future and the Role of Omni-Channel Payments in Driving Business Growth." WorldPay. 2015 https://www.worldpay.com/sites/default/files/WPUK-Om-ni-channel-payments-store-of-the-future.pdf

5. "Worldwide Retail and Ecommerce Sales: eMarketer's Estimates for 2016–2021" emarketer. July 18, 2017. https://www.emarketer.com/Report/Worldwide-Re-tail-Ecommerce-Sales-eMarketers-Esti-mates-20162021/2002090

6. Kemp, Simon. Digital in 2017: Global Overview. We are Social. January 24, 2017. https://wearesocial.com/special-reports/digital-in-2017-global-overview

CHAPTER 4

1. "Gartner Says 8.4 Billion Connected "Things" Will Be in Use in 2017, Up 31 Percent From 2016" Gartner Inc. February 7, 2017. https://www.gartner.com/newsroom/id/3598917

2. "From Stretched to Strengthened. Insights from the Global Chief Marketing Officer Study" IBM Institute for Business Media. March, 2014. http://www-01.ibm.com/common/ssi/cgi-bin/ssialias?subtype=XB&in-fotype=PM&appname=GBSE_GB_TI_USEN&htmlfid=GBE03593USEN&attach-ment=GBE03593USEN.PDF

CHAPTER 5

1. Elder, Robert. "Programmatic advertising is under review" Business Insider. January 31, 2017. http://www.businessinsider.com/pro-grammatic-advertising-under-review-2017-1

2. "IAB internet advertising revenue report" Interactive Advertising Bureau. April 2017. https://www.iab.com/wp-content/uploads/2016/04/IAB_Internet_Advertis-ing_Revenue_Report_FY_2016.pdf

3. "eMarketer Releases New Programmatic Advertising Estimates." eMarketer. April 18, 2017. https://www.emarketer.com/Article/eMarketer-Releases-New-Programmatic-Ad-vertising-Estimates/1015682

4. Daniel Newman , "The Top 8 IoT Trends For 2018" Forbes. December 19, 2017. https://www.forbes.com/sites/danielnew-man/2017/12/19/the-top-8-iot-trends-for-2018/#6993156d67f7

5. Olivier Blanchard "New Futurum Report: The 2017 IoT Business Integration Index" Futurum. September 19, 2017. https://futurumresearch.com/new-futurum-re-port-2017-iot-business-integration-index/

6. Lauren Hirsch. Amazon has big plans for Alexa ads in 2018; it's discussing options with P&G, Clorox and others. CNBC. January 2, 2018. https://www.cnbc.com/2018/01/02/amazon-alexa-is-opening-up-to-more-spon-sored-product-ads.html

CHAPTER 7

1. Akrur Barua. "Asia's retail spending boom: Shoppers go on a frenzy, and why not?" Deloitte Insights. March 28, 2017.https://www2.deloitte.com/insights/us/en/economy/asia-pacific-economic-outlook/2017/q2-asia-retail-spending-boom.html#endnote-4

2. "BrandZ Top 100 Most Valuable Brands 2017." Kantar Milward Brown. 2017. http://brandz.com/admin/uploads/files/BZ_Global_2017_Report.pdf

3. "Digital in Asia-Pacific in 2017" Kepios. September 28, 2017. https://kepios.com/blog/apac2017

4. https://econsultancy.com/blog/67692-the-best-apac-digital-marketing-stats-from-march-2016

5. "STUDY: 65 percent of U.S. consumers expect virtual reality will change the way people shop." WorldPay. May 25, 2017. https://globenewswire.com/news-release/2017/05/25/996096/0/en/STUDY-65-percent-of-U-S-consumers-expect-virtual-reality-will-change-the-way-people-shop.html

6. "The Asia Pacific Content Marketing Report 2016." Hubspot, Survey Monkey. 2016. https://offers.hubspot.com/the-asia-pacific-content-marketing-report-2016.

7. "eMarketer Expects Digital Video Viewership in Asia-Pacific to Increase by 10.3% This Year." eMarketer. January 16, 2017. https://www.emarketer.com/Article/eMarketer-Expects-Digital-Video-Viewership-Asia-Pacific-Increase-by-103-This-Year/1015037

8. Greeven, Mark and Wei Wei. "The rise of new technology giants from China" China Daily. October 10, 2017. http://www.chinadaily.com.cn/opinion/2017-10/10/content_33071873.htm

9. Wang, Helen H. "Why China Is Leading Us To The Future Of Commerce" Fortune. April 3, 2017. https://www.forbes.com/sites/helenwang/2017/04/03/why-china-is-leading-us-to-the-future-of-commerce/#51051de45d8e

10. "Number of smartphone users worldwide from 2014 to 2020 (in billions)" Statista. June 2016. https://www.statista.com/statistics/330695/number-of-smartphone-users-worldwide/

11. "Asia leads Burger King sales growth" Inside Retail Asia. August 5, 2016. https://insideretail.asia/2016/08/05/asia-leads-burger-king-sales-growth/

CHAPTER 8

1. Kantrowitz, Alex. "Kraft says it Rejects 75% to 85 % of Digital Ad Impressions due to Quality Concerns" AdAge. October 29, 2014. http://adage.com/article/datadriven-marketing/kraft-rejects-75-85-impressions-due-quality-issues/295635/

2. Joseph, Seb. "The state of the brand crackdown on media transparency" Digiday. August 17, 2017. https://digiday.com/marketing/state-brand-crackdown-media-transparency/

3. "ANA Study Finds Agency Compensation Models Shifting Away From Fees and Incentives" ANA. May 22, 2017. http://www.ana.net/content/show/id/44647

CHAPTER 10

1. Gazdik, Tanya. "Talent Crunch Plagues Marketing Industry." Marketing Daily. September 21, 2017. https://www.mediapost.com/publications/article/307685/talent-crunch-plagues-marketing-industry.html

2. Allen, Robert. "2017 Marketing Hiring Trends: Factors Shaping Demand for Marketing Talent" Smart Insights. May 17, 2017. https://www.smartinsights.com/managing-digital-marketing/2017-marketing-hiring-trends-factors-shaping-demand-marketing-talent/

3. "State of the Connected Customer" Salesforce. Oct 24, 2016. https://www.salesforce.com/blog/2016/10/state-of-connected-customer-2016.html

REFERENCES: FIGURES

CHAPTER 1

Figure 1: Mangles, Carolanne. "State of digital marketing 2017." Smart Insights. Last modified September 14, 2017.https://www.smartinsights.com/managing-digital-marketing/marketing-innovation/state-of-digital-marketing/attachment/state-of-digital-marketing-2017/.

Figure 2: "Q2 2017 Global Digital Statshot." We Are Social. Apr 11, 2017. https://www.slideshare.net/wearesocialsg/global-digital-statshot-q2-2017

Figure 3: "Cisco Visual Networking Index: Forecast and Methodology, 2016–2021." Cisco Systems. Last modified September 15, 2017. https://www.cisco.com/c/en/us/solutions/collateral/service-provider/visual-networking-index-vni/complete-white-paper-c11-481360.html

Figure 4: "Executives Championing Digital Transformation Efforts." Altimeter Group. 2014. https://www.slideshare.net/girujang/the-2014-state-of-digital-transformationaltimeter

Figure 5: "Executives Championing Digital Transformation Efforts." Altimeter Group. 2014. https://www.slideshare.net/girujang/the-2014-state-of-digital-transformationaltimeter

CHAPTER 2

Figure 6: "Digital disruption in Finance." Dear Media. June 19, 2015. https://www.slideshare.net/duvalunionconsulting/digital-disruption-in-finance

Figure 7: "Dell Technologies Research: 78% of Businesses Feel Threatened by Digital Start-ups" Dell Technologies. https://www.delltechnologies.com/en-us/press/unveiling-the-digital-transformation-index.htm

Figure 8: Boncheck, Mark, Cornfield, Gene. "There Are 4 Futures for CMOs (Some Better Than Others)" Harvard Business Review. September 18, 2017. https://hbr.org/2017/09/there-are-4-futures-for-cmos-some-better-than-others

Figure 9: "The Next Wave Of Digital Marketing Is Predictive." Forrester Consulting, Rocket Fuel. August, 2017. https://rocketfuel.com/wp-content/uploads/Forrester-TLP-The-Next-Wave-Of-Digital-Marketing-Is-Predictive-August-2017.pdf

CHAPTER 3

Figure 10: Satchu, Jamil; Chang, Connie. "Winning the CPG Zero-Sum Game by Uncovering Hidden Growth Pockets." IRI. February, 2017. https://www.iriworldwide.com/IRI/media/2017-Demand-Portfolio.pdf

Figure 11: "Winning at E-Commerce." R3. July 17, 2017. http://www.rthree.com/en/insight/detail/2ddJXEN.html

Figure 12: "Winning at E-Commerce." R3. July 17, 2017. http://www.rthree.com/en/insight/detail/2ddJXEN.html

Figure 13: Stevens, Laura. "Survey Shows Rapid Growth in Online Shopping." June 8, 2016. https://www.wsj.com/articles/survey-shows-rapid-growth-in-online-shopping-1465358582

CHAPTER 4

Figure 14: "Gartner Says 8.4 Billion Connected "Things" Will Be in Use in 2017, Up 31 Percent From 2016" Gartner Inc. February 7, 2017. https://www.gartner.com/newsroom/id/3598917

Figure 15: "From Stretched to Strengthened. Insights from the Global Chief Marketing Officer Study" IBM Institute for Business Media. March, 2014. http://www-01.ibm.com/common/ssi/cgi-bin/ssialias?subtype=XB&infotype=PM&appname=GBSE_GB_TI_USEN&htmlfid=GBE03593USEN&attachment=GBE03593USEN.PDF

Figure 16: "Big Data, Big Transformations." EMC Corporation. 2012. https://www.emc.com/collateral/white-papers/idg-bigdata-umbrella-wp.pdf

Figure 17: Yardley, Mike. "Chasing the Funnel, Part 1: Evolution of the Purchase Path." February 12, 2016. http://www.cmo.com/opinion/articles/2016/2/2/chasing-the-funnel-part-1-evolution-of-the-purchase-path.html#gs.vfp8znw

CHAPTER 5

Figure 18: "IAB internet advertising revenue report" Interactive Advertising Bureau. April 2017. https://www.iab.com/wp-content/uploads/2016/04/IAB_Internet_Advertising_Revenue_Report_FY_2016.pdf

Figure 19: Brinker, Scott. "Marketing Technology Landscape Supergraphic (2017): Martech 5000." Chiefmartec.com. May 10, 2017. https://chiefmartec.com/2017/05/marketing-technology-landscape-supergraphic-2017/

Figure 20: "eMarketer Releases New Programmatic Advertising Estimates." eMarketer. April 18, 2017. https://www.emarketer.com/Article/eMarketer-Releases-New-Programmatic-Advertising-Estimates/1015682

Figure 21: Desjardins, Jeff. "The Dominance of Google and Facebook in One Chart." Visual Caplitalist. December 9, 2016. www.visualcapitalist.com/dominance-google-and-facebook-one-chart/

Figure 22: "IOT Business Integration Index – 2017" Futurum Research. 2017. https://futurumresearch.com/product/iot-business-integration-index-2017/

Figure 23: Sourced from Internal R3 material

CHAPTER 6

Figure 24: Bauer, Thomas; Heller, Jason; Jacobs, Jeffrey, Schaffner, Rachel. "How to get the most from your agency relationships in 2017." Mckinsey & Company. February 2017. https://www.mckinsey.com/business-functions/marketing-and-sales/our-insights/how-to-get-the-most-from-your-agency-relationships-in-2017

Figure 25: Paull, Greg. "Integration 40." R3. February 18, 2015. http://r3integration40.com/

CHAPTER 7

Figure 26: Barua, Akrur. "Asia's retail spending boom: Shoppers go on a frenzy, and why not?" Deloitte Insights. March 28, 2017. https://www2.deloitte.com/insights/us/en/economy/asia-pacific-economic-outlook/2017/q2-asia-retail-spending-boom.html#endnote-4

Figure 27: "BrandZ Top 100 Most Valuable Brands 2017." Kantar Milward Brown. 2017. http://brandz.com/admin/uploads/files/BZ_Global_2017_Report.pdf

Figure 28, 29 & 30: "Digital in Asia-Pacific in 2017" Kepios. September 28, 2017. https://kepios.com/blog/apac2017

Figure 31: "eMarketer Releases New Programmatic Advertising Estimates." eMarketer. April 18, 2017. https://www.emarketer.com/Article/eMarketer-Releases-New-Programmatic-Advertising-Estimates/1015682

Figure 32: "Q2 2017 Global Digital Statshot." We Are Social. Apr 11, 2017. https://www.slideshare.net/wearesocialsg/global-digital-statshot-q2-2017

Figure 33: Barua, Akrur. "Asia's retail spending boom: Shoppers go on a frenzy, and why not?" Deloitte Insights. March 28, 2017. https://www2.deloitte.com/insights/us/en/economy/asia-pacific-economic-outlook/2017/q2-asia-retail-spending-boom.html#endnote-4

CHAPTER 8

Figure 34: "IAB Programmatic Revenue Report 2014 Results." Interactive Advertising Bureau. July 2015. https://www.slideshare.net/RTBforum/iab-programmatic-revenue-report-2014-results

Figure 35: "China's Programmatic Landscape" R3. October 2015. http://www.rthree.com/en/insight/detail/bafRXC.html

Figure 36: "Infographic | The 10 Most Important Number from the ANA's Media Transparency Report." R3. June 15, 2016. http://www.rthree.com/en/insight/detail/945JTvP.html

Figure 37: Paull, Greg. "Global 40: A report by R3 on 40 of the world's most enduring relationships between marketers and their agencies" October, 2016.

Figure 38: Senior Management Involvement "ANA Study Finds Agency Compensation Models Shifting Away From Fees and Incentives" ANA. May 22, 2017.

CHAPTER 9:

Figure 39: "Understanding the Sales Funnel in 2016." Mind & Metrics. February 28, 2016. https://mindandmetrics.com/the-evolution-of-the-sales-funnel/

Figure 40: Kayyali, Basel; Kelly, Steve; Pawar, Madhu. "Why digital transformation should be a strategic priority for health insurers." McKinsey & Company. May, 2016. https://www.mckinsey.com/industries/healthcare-systems-and-services/our-insights/why-digital-transformation-should-be-a-strategic-priority-for-health-insurers

Figure 41: Burney, Kara. "3 Ways to Future-Proof Your Marketing Team Structure." Track Maven. 2017. https://trackmaven.com/blog/future-proof-marketing-team-structure/

Figure 42: Benson-Armer, Richard; Gast, Arne; van Dam, Nick. "Learning at the speed of business." Mckinsey & Company. May, 2016. https://www.mckinsey.com/business-functions/organization/our-insights/learning-at-the-speed-of-business

CHAPTER 10:

Figure 43: Gazdik, Tanya. "Talent Crunch Plagues Marketing Industry." *Marketing Daily.* September 21, 2017. https://www.mediapost.com/publications/article/307685/talent-crunch-plagues-marketing-industry.html

Figure 44: Allen, Robert. "2017 Marketing Hiring Trends: Factors Shaping Demand for Marketing Talent" Smart Insights. May 17, 2017. https://www.smartinsights.com/managing-digital-marketing/2017-marketing-hiring-trends-factors-shaping-demand-marketing-talent/